# SMOKE SCREEN

# SMOKE SCREEN

How a Good Kid Got Hooked on Drugs and
What He and His Family Did About It

## Betsy Tice White

ABINGDON PRESS

Nashville

# SMOKE SCREEN

*Copyright © 1989 by Betsy T. White*

This book is printed on acid-free paper.

**Library of Congress Cataloging-in-Publication Data**

WHITE, BETSY TICE, 1936–
   Smoke screen:how a good kid got hooked on drugs and
what he and his family did about it/Betsy Tice White
      p.   cm.
Bibliography: p.

**ISBN 0-687-38740-X** (alk. paper)

1. Teenagers—United States—Drug use—Case studies.
2. Narcotic addicts—Rehabilitation—United States—Case studies.
3. Narcotic addicts—United States—Family relationships—Case studies.
I. Title.
HV5824.Y68W48   1989
362.2'92'0924—dc19                                    88-37593
[B]                                                          CIP

The epigram on the dedication page is Copyright © by Martin Luther King, Jr., and Estate of Martin Luther King, Jr. Reprinted by permission of Joan Daves.

MANUFACTURED BY THE PARTHENON PRESS
NASHVILLE, TENNESSEE, UNITED STATES OF AMERICA

For Henry, who hoped;
Thornton, who tried;
and John, whose surrender is triumph

———

*In a real sense all life is interrelated. All men are caught in an inescapable network of mutuality, tied in a single garment of destiny. Whatever affects one directly affects all indirectly. I can never be what I ought to be until you are what you ought to be, and you can never be what you ought to be until I am what I ought to be. This is the interrelated structure of reality.*

—*Rev. Martin Luther King, Jr.*

_____*Smoke Screen* is a document of denial by the family, the community, and a college, as related to the drug dependency of a young man. It reveals the intense reaction of a mother and son and the family triangles which exist when excessive use of alcohol or other drugs results in serious dysfunction of an individual, accompanied by denial on the part of all persons who have a primary relationship with that individual.

Eventually the parents confront the son and place him in a treatment program which requires family participation. As the son returns to a drug-free life, the parents begin to face the fact that they had focused on the son to the extent of ignoring their own needs, and they slowly begin to rebuild their marriage.

Although there is basic improvement for all members of the family, the evidence indicates a glaring truth. When a child is on drugs or alcohol, parents desperately need to get the focus off the child and seek help for themselves, as suggested in the final chapter. The book makes the family triangle come alive, and reading it can give parents insight into their own struggle with children whose lives seriously disrupt the whole family.

—Joseph L. Kellermann
Charlotte, North Carolina

# CONTENTS

# ACKNOWLEDGMENTS

*T*his book owes its existence to many special people. My gratitude to them is boundless; words are a feeble return of thanks. Standing staunchly behind me were Edith Brice, Arlyn Firkins Bruccoli, Mary Jane Burns, Beverly Cosby, Peg Cox, Astrid and John Hansen, David Hiers, Betsy Latimer Jaffe, Lisa Joyner, Joel Keys, Mary Ellen Lee, Michael Marshall, Deldon Anne McNeely, Michael Newman, and Herb and Mary Jane Smith.

Thanks are also due Stephen Apthorp, Janet Johnson, Vernon Johnson, John Killinger, Marcia Lawton, Gerald May, Robert Meyners, Jack Mills, John Sanford, Sheldon Vanauken, Janet Vultee, Sharon Wegscheider-Cruse, Linda Weiner, and Lyon Williams.

Encouragement from Rosemarie Axton, Donald Brophy, Glenn Busch, Peter Houck, Jack Mumey, Philip Parham, John and Verna Price, Ruth Reynolds, and Mary Ross mattered enormously.

And without the generosity of Gwen and Jody Kellermann, I never could have brought it off.

I remember with deeply felt thanks my mother, who understood the healing power of God and A.A.; my father, who taught me to endure; my brother, the first chemically dependent person I cared about; and my husband and children, for their infinite loyalty and love.

_____ *T*his is a story about a boy named John, who nearly died as a result of drugs and alcohol before he was old enough to buy a legal drink. For far too long, no one in John's world realized what was wrong with him or how sick he really was.

John's parents—Bob and I—are good citizens, hard-working, well-educated, churchgoing upholders of family stability and traditional American values. We love each other, and we love our children. We have worked hard at being good parents and have tried to guide our children into responsible, healthy directions. We did all the "right" things.

But from the time our middle child, John, was thirteen years old, we found ourselves living with a teenage Jekyll and Hyde. Throughout John's adolescence, we were unable to recognize that John was suffering from the disease called chemical dependency. At various times we thought he must be sociopathic, mentally ill, or inherently evil. At other times, his winsomeness convinced us that we were to blame for his difficulties and had sorely misjudged our son.

None of the counselors or clergy we consulted understood what was happening either and could only suggest approaches by which we might function better as a family. Using their methods was like trying to put out a four-alarm fire with a water pistol.

Bob and I agonized about our boy as we endured entanglements with the police, the courts, and, seemingly, the whole of decent society. We felt powerless as John walled himself behind an emotional barrier, which finally no one, not even he himself, could penetrate. And eventually, we who loved him found that barrier preferable to his emotional firestorms.

Because of John's disease, our respectable middle-class suburban home became the scene of endless conflict, shouting and shoving matches, and all-night anguish. Our family circle, which should have served as a peaceful haven from the knocks and bruises of the outside world, was instead continually clouded by wordless fears and unrelenting emotional pain. Every member of our household suffered torment in the wake of John's disease. His younger brother and older sister came to fear, avoid, and almost hate him.

Bob and I kept telling ourselves it was just a very difficult adolescent rebellion, that things were bound to get better. We saw it all happening, and yet we were frighteningly unaware that John was on a fast downhill slide toward destruction and death.

Then just in time, and to our family's everlasting gratitude, a friend shared with us some all-important knowledge that saved John's life. Here we share that same knowledge with you, believing our story may also be your family's story, or that of a relative or friend. Chemical dependency is epidemic in America today. One of every ten adult Americans is addicted to alcohol or other mind-altering drugs. *And one of every four adolescents abuses alcohol, other drugs, or both.*

John is among the fortunate few, for he received the specific help he needed in time to save his life. He is no longer an antisocial outlaw or a raging suicidal delinquent. He is a fine man and a good citizen, healthy and intelligent, with a deep feeling for his fellow human beings. He was never a bad person; he was a good kid with a fatal disease, which no one recognized until it was almost too late.

There are several million adolescent Americans just like John. If telling his story can save one youngster's life or help one parent find the way back to rewarding existence, it will have been worth telling. If this is your story too, we hope you will use our account of healing and reconciliation to guide you back home, where you belong.

# SMOKE SCREEN

# A Chemical Society, a Good Family, and a Problem Kid

_____ The parents of America's adolescents are haunted by the nightmare specter of drugs, with good reason. The tumultuous 1960s are gone but not forgotten. We are still reaping their harvest. Our newspapers and magazines are full of stories about the multibillion-dollar drug industry, and alcohol is a pervasive fact of life. It's a rare social event that doesn't include a baggie or a bottle. Television and movies have long featured the serving of cocktails and wine; now they portray matter-of-fact consumption of other drugs as well. Pot, cocaine, uppers and downers are everywhere. Anyone—teenagers and even younger children—can obtain them easily.

Much of the music favored by adolescents contains many allusions to drugs; parents either don't hear or don't understand these allusions, or perhaps believe them harmless. But young people flock to rock concerts where drug-taking is open and virtually universal; most parents have no idea what these events are like. Parents who leave town frequently return to find there has been a party and the place is trashed. Alcohol-related automobile accidents are a leading cause of death among teens. Adolescent suicide is at an all-time high, and it is estimated that 70 percent of such deaths are associated with substance abuse.

Many drinking and drugging teens cease to function academically, skip school, nod off in class, clash with one authority figure after another, counting the minutes until they are able to escape from adult supervision into self-administered anesthesia. In the absence of intervention, most such kids eventually drop out of school to take up dead-end jobs or pursue aimless, drug- or alcohol-centered lives, going nowhere and no longer caring. Others may be smart enough to stay in school, but they're generally apathetic, lack motivation, and just go through the motions, performing far below their potential.

Nor is the problem confined to kids. Adults pop pills and go for the gusto, too. Many of us drink to excess, smoke pot, and snort coke. It seems that almost every week we hear of another celebrity from the entertainment or sports world in trouble with alcohol or drugs. Legions of youngsters grow up in homes with substance-abusing parents, suffering untold physical abuse and emotional trauma. Our highways are littered with the wreckage caused by mind-altering substances. Is it any wonder we're scared for our kids?

I too was a frightened parent. I had grown up under the shadow of an older brother's alcoholism, and though he no longer lived at home, I was aware of the affect of addiction on a family's peace and sanity. When our own three children—Susan, John, and Mike—came along, my worst fear was that they might become hooked on alcohol and other drugs. Determined that the miserable old story would not be replayed in my household, I resolutely set out to keep it from happening.

Bob and I worked hard at being good parents, striving to establish an atmosphere of acceptance, security, and love. We took our youngsters to Sunday school, church youth groups, Scouts, and every other place we knew of where moral values were upheld and responsible living taught. We spoke often about the harmful effects of drugs, including alcohol, from the time they were old enough to understand the words.

Both Bob and I had been raised in homes that were adamantly teetotal. In my home, this was a reaction to my brother's behavior; Bob's family based its stance on religious grounds. Such an upbringing sometimes makes alcohol more attractive, so we decided to accept alcohol in moderation in our home and social life. By eliminating the lure of the forbidden, we hoped to teach our children to be sensible drinkers. At home we occasionally allowed them sips of beer or wine at dinner, assuming they would learn in this way to use alcohol thoughtfully and responsibly. We believed we were setting a good example.

As our kids grew, we spent much time together. Bob took the boys fishing and hunting. I taught all three to cook and enjoyed their help in the kitchen. We went on family hikes and picnics. Everyone in the household learned to play a bluegrass instrument; our family band was great fun. When I took a part-time job, I made sure I was home by 3:00 P.M. for that important after-school time with my children. Bob's medical practice occasionally called him out in the evenings, but he was generally home at nights and on weekends.

We both worked with youth organizations. Bob headed up a Webelos den. I played the piano for the youth choir at church and helped with the young people's group. We went to PTA meetings and kept in touch with our children's teachers and principals. We volunteered for community service, believing we owed the world something in return for our privileged life.

In the early years, our three seemed model kids. They were bright, lively, and good-natured. They did extremely well in school and behaved as well as others their age. They took an active part in church life and had plenty of friends. They seemed to be growing up healthy and free.

But an ominous change began around John's twelfth birthday. Until then he had been an honor-roll student with a variety of hobbies: magic tricks and model building, coin and stamp collecting, dinosaurs and astronomy. He loved to read, especially stories about Robin Hood, the adventures of Sherlock Holmes, and the Tolkien trilogy. He played a five-string banjo amazingly well.

Both John and Mike, ten, enjoyed sports. When a soccer league was formed, they joined eagerly and practiced after school twice a week. I picked them up on my way home from work. One afternoon when I drove up to the soccer field, Mike was waiting alone.

"Mike, where's John?"

Mike climbed into the car. "He told the coach he had to leave early and went to Stu Sutton's house. Are you going to punish him?"

"Well, I don't know. There may be a perfectly good explanation. We'll have to see. Mrs. Sutton teaches school, so she's probably not home."

I drove to the Suttons'. Sure enough, John was there with Stu, but Mrs. Sutton was not. I told John to get in the car.

"Son, you aren't to go anywhere without permission," I reminded him as we headed home. "You must stay at soccer practice until I come for you. Anyway, Mrs. Sutton is still at work and you know you're not allowed to visit friends unless at least one parent is home."

"Okay," John answered indifferently.

I let Mrs. Sutton know what had happened, then forgot about it until a week later, when the same thing happened again. The second time, I was pretty steamed when I picked John up, and that night Bob and I agreed to ground him for a week. No friends could come over to play, and he was forbidden to leave home except for school and soccer.

We thought the problem was solved. Things went on smoothly for a month. Then as I parked beside the playing field once again, I spotted John and Stu Sutton coming through the hedge at the far end. Mike spilled the beans before John made it to the car.

"Mom, John never stays at practice any more. He leaves before the coach gets here and goes somewhere with Stu. They come back right before you pick us up."

"Michael, why didn't you tell me this before?"

"John said he'd beat me up if I told."

"Does he leave every time?"

"Yep Every single time, ever since you let him off of being grounded."

A sick feeling came over me. John had been successfully deceiving me for weeks. Was I losing control of a twelve-year-old? Bob and I talked it over and decided to ground John for two weeks this time, after the stiffest lecture ever.

For the remainder of soccer season, I took it upon myself to leave work an hour early and sit in my car beside the athletic field, to make sure John stayed through practice. For the first time, I allowed his behavior to modify my own life pattern.

The problem became chronic in the weeks and months

that followed. John misbehaved again and again in a variety of ways. We lectured and grounded him repeatedly, in a desperate effort to maintain control of our suddenly wayward child. He tried more than once to get even with his little brother for telling on him. Conflicts between all our children increased.

Susie was then sixteen, enjoying high school and looking forward to college. Mike was in the fourth grade. At the slightest provocation from either sibling, John had fits of temper, screamed, shoved, scratched, pounded. They fought back, but our strong older boy could really hurt them.

Bob and I stepped in repeatedly to keep the peace. Each time, we made John confess his wrongs and apologize. There was little sincerity in those forced apologies, but he went through the motions. With similar urging, Susie and Mike told him grudgingly it was okay, often before the tears were dry on their cheeks.

Then there began to be trouble at school—worrisome phone calls from teachers, then from the principal.

"Mrs. White? I'm calling to report that John has been causing a great deal of trouble at school recently."

"I'm very sorry to hear it. What has he done?"

"He's been generally disruptive and disobedient. I'm keeping him an hour after school every day this week."

"Thank you for letting us know. His father and I will certainly speak to John about this."

Every few days it was something new: He flushed a pear from his lunch down the toilet to stop it up; he switched on the record player whenever the teacher turned her back; he constantly talked and disturbed others. With each such occurrence, John was punished at school and also at home—by grounding or withholding his allowance. But John's basic behavior remained unaltered. He just spent a lot more time staying after school or confined to his room or yard.

And then a much more serious difficulty arose. John came home from school one day with a new assignment.

"Mom, I have to write a research paper. My English teacher says I have to go to the university library to do it. Can you take me there?"

"Why, sure, honey, if that's what you're supposed to do."

I thought it was wonderful for John to be learning to do library research as early as sixth grade. I was happy to drop him off at the campus then and many times afterward. He usually went with a couple of friends, stayed an hour or two, and met me outside the library at 5:30.

As I waited there in the car at 5:45 one day, wondering where John could be, a patrol car parked in back of me. A uniformed officer got out and approached.

"Pardon me, ma'am, are you Mrs. White?"

"Yes, is something wrong?"

"Well, ma'am, I'll have to ask you to follow me over to Campus Security. We have your son and another boy in custody. The security chief wants to see both sets of parents right away."

I was frightened. As the policeman pulled his car around mine, I spied John in the back seat. He had slid down so low as to be barely visible, but he gazed directly at me, and I'd never imagined a human being could look so desperate. His face was deathly pale, his eyes panicky— the picture of someone feeling trapped and sick. His friend Brett Saunders cowered on the other side of the seat, looking very much the same.

I followed the patrol car slowly through the campus. My fear turned to anger, mingled with shame. Whatever John was accused of, I was sure he had done it.

Why had he begun to cause so much trouble? Why couldn't he be a "good" boy like everyone else's child?

# CHAPTER TWO

# *Probation, Pot, and Placation*

_____*A*t the security office John and Brett waited on a bench in the hall. I followed the officer into an inner room. There I was introduced to Sergeant Justis of the city police and Captain Martin of Campus Security. The boys' mischief had been in progress for some time—all those afternoons when I had assumed John was doing research at the library.

"Several weeks ago we found something strange in the bill-changing machines on campus," Captain Martin told me. He held out a black-and-white facsimile of a dollar bill. "Somebody was putting photocopies of dollar bills in and getting quarters back. The amounts taken were bigger and bigger each week—several hundred dollars. We spoke to the city police, and they'd picked up the same thing at a carwash near the university and at a downtown parking lot."

Sergeant Justis took up the story. "We decided to stake out the machine on campus that had been hit most often, in a dorm near the library. Our man hid in a closet. When someone showed up and started feeding in a stack of bills, he stepped out and grabbed him."

"We'd expected to pick up college students," said

Captain Martin, "or maybe someone from town. We certainly didn't expect a couple of juvenile counterfeiters."

"What happens next?"

"John's father needs to come. Brett's parents are already on their way. As I say, this is actually counterfeiting, and we're required to call in the United States Treasury agent. It'll take him a couple of hours to get here. I'm sorry, but you'll have to wait until he comes."

*Why is all this happening to me?* I was thinking angrily as I dialed our home number, told Bob briefly about the trouble, then hung up and waited for him to arrive. What in the world were we going to do with this boy?

Scenes from the recent past flashed through my mind. When John had met me in front of the library, he was often carrying a package from one of the shops near the campus—a new T-shirt or a record album. Once it was the biggest submarine sandwich I'd ever seen. A week earlier, he'd come home sporting a new digital watch, giving a plausible explanation—he had saved up his birthday money and earnings from jobs around the house and babysitting. Now it all became clear: Those things were bought with stolen money.

Brett's mother and father came in, looking very worried. We knew them slightly. They were new in our town—good people, conscientious parents. They looked as if they felt every bit as wretched as I did. Bob arrived soon afterward. Just having him there beside me made the situation a little more bearable. We all waited in silence for two long hours.

The Treasury agent finally arrived. He conferred with the other officers, then called us in. His manner was pleasant, but there was no nonsense about him.

"You parents and boys must first understand there's

been a violation of federal law. John and Brett, you've been counterfeiting U.S. currency."

I could already hear the cellblock door clanging shut.

Apparently reading my thoughts, he went on. "Even though federal law makes no distinction between adult crime and juvenile crime, I'm not interested in sending thirteen-year-olds to federal prison. I have teenage youngsters myself. I think you boys deserve a chance to straighten up before you get into worse trouble. My main interest is to convince you that the federal law is *very* serious business." He paused to let his words sink in.

"I've talked it over with the officers here, and we've agreed to let the city's juvenile court system take over this case. Sergeant Justis will follow up. This will satisfy the federal authorities, and I hope it will serve everybody's good."

Our relief was boundless. The situation was not ideal, but it was much better than it might have been.

Within a few weeks John and Brett were sitting on a hard bench again, this time in a closed hearing before a juvenile court judge. Four sad and embarrassed parents were there too. The judge heard the facts of the case, then gave us an opportunity to speak. Brett's mother and I left our sons' defense to their fathers.

When Bob's turn came, he got to his feet. "Your honor, since this thing has happened, John's mother and I have decided—that is, if you approve—to enroll John in a church-supported boarding school. We believe a challenging school and strict environment will get him straightened out."

"Reasonable enough," the judge replied. "I'm willing to go along with that. Since this is a first offense and you parents are taking a firm hand, I'll make no adjudication yet in regard to delinquency. I'm giving these boys one more chance, putting them on probation for a year. Now, if they should violate their probation agreement or commit a second offense, there'll be no further question of leniency."

Once again waves of relief washed over me. Bob and I looked forward to turning John over to someone else's authority for the next school year. We hoped a more stimulating academic environment would have good effect. *Our* disciplinary approach wasn't working. Perhaps someone else's would.

We were relying on a change of scenery to reform John. We thought he needed a tougher school, new friends, more structure. We were in for a crashing disappointment, because the source of the problem was not the environment, but John himself. In the world of alcohol and drug rehabilitation, a change of environment is known as the "geographic cure," and it *never* works.

Ted, John's probation officer, was a personable, intelligent young man who did everything possible to get John back on the straight and narrow. He spent time with him, encouraged him, constantly reminded him how fortunate he was to have parents who cared for him and were giving him every opportunity to succeed. Ted urged John to do everything expected of him, both at home and at school in the coming fall. We hoped John was listening. There was no way to tell.

The terms of the probation agreement required that the boys get summer jobs. John went to work on a farm, and every penny of his earnings went to repay the money he'd stolen. By summer's end, the debt was cleared entirely, with a little left over. John behaved pretty well, but it was like watching the burning fuse of a very large firecracker. We had a strong sense that he might "go off " again at any time. I could hardly wait for him to be safely installed in boarding school, under the watchful eye of a stern headmaster.

And so John left home for the first time at age thirteen, to enter ninth grade in a boarding school two hundred miles away. He didn't seem to mind saying good-bye. After he'd gone we felt generally relieved, but sometimes I had misgivings. Was he too young to be fending for himself?

We heard little from John. His faculty advisor reported he was making a good start. We visited the school on Parents' Weekend, and John was functioning pretty well, as far as we could tell. He enjoyed a restaurant dinner with us and asked us to drive him to the nearby mountains to go hiking in the woods. Our greatest concern was that he had made no close friends, but we trusted time to take care of that. We left for home feeling generally optimistic.

When John came home for Thanksgiving he appeared troubled. Susie, back from her freshman year at college, picked up on it right away. He was restless, irritable, and depressed; yet he would never say exactly what was bothering him. As we all sat around a cozy fire after our Thanksgiving dinner, Bob probed for information.

"Son, do you get along with your roommate?"

"I hate him," said John vehemently. "He's a rich brat and a snob, and he hates me too."

"It surely can't be that bad. What makes you think he hates you?"

"For one thing, he makes fun of my music all the time." John was developing a taste for heavy-metal rock. "He likes beach music, which I can't stand, and one day while I was out of my room somebody took my new Van Halen album and scratched it up so I can't even play it. I know he did it. Nobody else was on the hall."

"What about your counselor?" asked Susie. "I'll bet he'd help you work it out."

"It's not just that one thing," John declared intensely. "It's *everything*! Everybody hates my music, and they hate my clothes and make fun of them all the time. The others all have preppie rich-boy clothes, and I have J. C. Penney. Almost every night they take my bed apart and stand it up in a corner, and I have to put it back together again and make it up before I can go to sleep."

He was on the verge of tears. "They all say I'm a weirdo!" His voice broke and he finally blurted out, "They call me the school freak!"

To us, "freak" meant "misfit." To the youngsters who applied the label, it may have meant "drug user." John himself may not have been aware of this meaning, or his anguish may have been a cry for help at this early stage.

We didn't know how much was exaggeration and how much was truth, but John's pain was certainly real. Mike listened in sympathetic silence. Susie, Bob, and I suspected we hadn't heard the whole story. We probed and probed but got nowhere. Finally Bob gave up the effort with a yawn.

"Well, son, hospital rounds come mighty early in the morning. I'm calling it a day for now, but I'd like to talk about this some more. How about tomorrow?"

"Okay, Dad, fine." John looked defeated.

Susan and I were reluctant to leave it at that. We sat up with John until 2:00 A.M., questioning, rehashing, struggling to pinpoint the reasons for his wretchedness. He merely told us again and again that he was miserable in every way. He begged to leave school and come home.

"Mom, I'll do *anything*, anything you tell me to, if you'll just let me come back home!" His suffering was pitiable.

"All right, John. I'll speak to Daddy about it tomorrow

and ask him to think it over. But for now, we have to get some sleep."

He seemed satisfied at last.

"Thank you, Mom. I love you." He hugged Susie and me before he headed upstairs.

Susie was still thinking after John left us.

"Mom, I know how terrible it is to feel homesick. Maybe that's what's really wrong. I felt like that when I went to camp. Will you beg Daddy to let John come back home? I don't think John's making all this up."

"Don't worry. I will. I don't think he's making it up either. I feel sorry for him too."

The kids slept late the next day. At breakfast I put the question to Bob.

"How would you feel about letting John come home?"

"I'm totally against it," he said decisively. "Have you forgotten what it was like here before he left? The kids fighting all the time, John's temper fits, constant difficulties at school, not to mention trouble with the law—I don't know about you, but I'm not ready to take all that on again."

"But, honey, he promises to do everything we tell him, if we'll just let him come back. I really pity the boy. He seems so miserable. Won't you think about it?"

"I'll think about it. But that doesn't mean I'm changing my mind."

Bob appreciated the peace of our household with John and Susie away. So did I, but John was working powerfully on my sympathy, something he knew how to do very well indeed.

He soon had everyone in the family involved in his campaign. Tender-hearted Susan wrote home from college, pleading with her dad. Brother Mike said staunchly, "I'd hate that school, if it's like John says it is. If you wouldn't let *me* come home, I'd run away!"

With all of us working on him, Bob finally softened. One evening during the Christmas vacation he gave his answer.

"John, I've made my decision. I don't want you to get the idea you can quit something just because it's unpleasant, so I'm going to insist that you finish out the year at boarding school."

Poor John's face fell.

Bob continued. "However, if you *do* finish out the year and do well . . . " John drew in his breath expectantly. "I'm willing to let you come back home and go to high school here—provided you behave yourself absolutely and do every single thing we expect of you."

John let out a whoop of joy, pounced on his dad and hugged and kissed him, crossed his heart, offered to swear on the Bible and anything else that would convince us of his intention to straighten up.

"Dad, you won't be sorry," he vowed earnestly. "You can count on me!"

I felt satisfied, because everybody was happy. In those days, I worked *very* hard at keeping everybody happy.

Many problems plagued John that whole year. His allowance was never enough, he said. When he left for school after the Christmas holidays, Bob gave him $20. We telephoned two days later to see how he was settling in after the vacation.

"I'm doing okay, but I need some money."

Bob hit the ceiling. "What?! You left here day before yesterday with a twenty-dollar bill! Surely you haven't spent $20 already!"

"I think somebody stole it, Dad. When I looked in my

wallet, it was gone. You can send me a check, can't you?"

"I don't believe this, John," said Bob. "Go right now and look again carefully in your wallet, all your pockets, your jacket, everywhere. Call me right back to let me know whether you've found it."

John phoned back, reporting no sign of the money. Grumbling, Bob agreed to send him a check.

John's first-semester grades came, and they were good enough for the headmaster's honor roll. But he still had almost no friends.

At spring break John was still complaining of not having enough money. We sat down together and listed a typical week's expenditures; it came to about $12. We always sent him $20. He said he went to an occasional movie, sometimes shared a pizza, and bought snacks in the school's canteen—nothing else.

I was truly bewildered. "Son, I just don't understand this."

"Somebody's stealing money in the dorm," he told me with a straight face. "A friend of mine had $250 stolen out of his room right before break. I think they've been taking my money too."

"Well, John, keep your wallet locked up in your closet. That's the only sensible thing to do."

A fleeting question did pass through my mind: What was a boy that age doing with $250?

The critical point of truth—a truth of which Bob and I had no inkling—was that John had been drawn into the chemical culture. He had begun to get drunk and high on pot regularly. Most of the boys at his school had plenty of spending money, and alcohol and other drugs were easy to get. Alienated, confused, and desperately lonely, John discovered that marijuana and alcohol would relieve those painful feelings. For the rest of that miserable school year he dosed himself regularly with those anesthetics.

During his troubled Thanksgiving stay at home, John may have been hoping we would realize the difficulty he was in and help him find a way out. He may have been voicing a cry for help; if so, it went unrecognized. We weren't mind readers. John was already in bondage to his guilty secret. Within a few months of smoking his first joint, he had found himself walled off in a prison of his own making, blocked from any movement toward growth and wholeness.

As summer began John came happily home to stay. He completed his year of probation to the satisfaction of the court and signed up to work on the farm again. We were glad to have him occupied.

Determined for John to learn to manage his money better, I took him to the bank to open a checking account so that he could deposit his weekly earnings. I didn't know a co-signature could be required on any checks drawn against the account. I gave my fourteen-year-old so much rope, figuratively speaking, that I was helping him to hang himself.

Early in the summer John was thoroughly agreeable. He got up cheerfully, caught his ride to work, and got home in the late afternoon in a surprisingly amiable frame of mind for someone who had labored all day in the broiling sun. There was a secret explanation for his good humor: John got high every afternoon on the way home with the older boy who drove the farm truck. We hadn't the slightest suspicion, nor did we know the signs to look for. After a shower, a short rest, and a good supper, he was ready to visit a friend or take in a movie. He always had money for entertainment; he put his paycheck in the bank faithfully every week.

When the first month's bank statement came in, we had a battle royal. John's bookkeeping was lousy. He'd written checks without stubbing them in; there were several to "cash" for $20 and $30. His balance hovered barely above zero.

"John, what are you doing with all your money? I don't understand this. A few movies and an album now and then don't add up to that much."

"Mom, it's *my* money," he came back testily. "*I* worked for it, you know, and *this* year I can do anything I want to with it. Just quit hassling me! Get off my back! I can handle things just fine."

"Son, the idea was for you to learn to manage your money. I don't think you've done that."

"You drive me crazy!" he exploded. "You're always trying to run my life! This is *my* money. It doesn't have anything to do with you!"

"Son, it does have to do with me. The bank required me to sign for you because you're a minor. If you overdraw your account or mess up, I'm responsible."

"Okay, then! I won't have a bank account. I'll just keep my money in my room and take out what I want to spend."

"We're not going along with that. We want you to learn to be accountable for your money."

"Account for it yourself, dammit!"

John stormed up to his room and slammed the door; we didn't see him again until suppertime. When he did come downstairs, Bob made him apologize. I accepted his apology without comment.

This nasty scene was repeated the following month, with John even more hostile. The checks made out to cash were larger—$60 and $70. My questions were never answered satisfactorily, and Bob left the matter entirely up to me. It still didn't occur to me to require a cosignature on John's checks; even if I had thought of it, his wrath probably would have been enough to keep me from standing my ground.

John bought himself a really good stereo and added to his album collection every week. I told myself that must be where the money was going. But I knew it really wasn't so. Something was very wrong. I didn't know how to set things right, and I was afraid to try. John had undermined my self-confidence. He was now in control.

Things became worse. John's good mood of the afternoon now lasted no longer than an hour or so. By suppertime we never knew how he would behave. He might be giggling and joking; an hour later he might turn sullen and uncommunicative.

Our evening meal, a family time we usually looked forward to, became a dreaded ordeal. John was irritable, scornful, rude. We talked around him and avoided all comments or questions that might rub him the wrong way. If, in spite of our caution, something did provoke an outburst, he'd shove his chair back violently, stamp upstairs to his room, slam the door, and lock it behind him.

John's unpredictable moods and isolation became a pattern. Our entire household began to accept this unhealthy way of life. We couldn't see any other way to survive.

We couldn't see through that locked door, either. If we could, we'd have seen John take down a framed picture from its nail, reach into a hole he'd made in the wall, take out papers and a bag of pot, and deftly roll a joint. A few puffs lifted him to the level of no-feeling he craved. He lay on the bed smoking, listening to his records, floating away. A big electric fan in the window blew the smoke outside, so suspicions were not aroused downstairs. Eyedrops counteracted the redness of his eyes, and when he appeared downstairs an hour or so later, he was Mr. Cool again, calm and composed, pleasant and polite.

This transformation was bewildering. Every time it happened, I mistrusted my memory of the fury that had gone before. John could be so nice when he chose! He kept us alternating between despair and hope, frustration and resolution. Riding such an emotional roller coaster was exhausting, but we didn't know how to get off.

When we asked where he was going, in the evening, his replies became vague and evasive.

"I'm not sure. Chris and I might go to the mall, or we might go over to somebody's house."

"Whose house?"

"I'm not sure. Maybe David's, maybe Chris's, maybe Brett's." It became harder and harder to pin him down. If I phoned where he had said he would be, the parent answering would say no, the boys weren't there, they were at someone else's house. If I called that place, I got another story from another parent.

We told John firmly that he must let us know exactly where he was going every time he left the house.

"No problem!" he said cheerfully. "I'll call you when I get there! G'bye!" But he could never "remember" to phone.

It was like soccer practice all over again, except that now John got around town on his own, walking, hitchhiking, catching rides with friends. He was a free agent. Any attempt to tighten up on him was like trying to lasso an eel.

We could find no way to control him. If we grounded him, he behaved so well for the next few days, we would relent, thinking we'd been too harsh. But there was always a next offense, and a next, and a next.

Fall came, finally, and with it John's return to public high school. He got by with a minimum of study. Most evenings he stretched out on his bed with his stereo headphones, always behind that locked door. He started to smoke tobacco, but never in our presence—only in his room. We didn't like it, but we couldn't find a way to stop it. Bribes didn't work. He made promises, took the rewards, and continued to smoke; the tobacco smoke camouflaged the pungent marijuana fumes.

Bob and I drew on the latest books on bringing up teenagers. "The teen years are hard." "Adolescence is very painful." "Be patient." "Kids have to rebel against their parents from time to time. It's part of growing up." "Teens need time to themselves." "It's important to respect a youngster's privacy."

We wanted to be good parents; we obeyed the so-called experts, and our laissez-faire stance suited John fine.

Using his magic potions with regularity, he avoided the growth in relationships and the emotional adjustments that are essential in a healthy adolescence. Our failure to call John back from his self-imposed isolation, our inability to make him rejoin the family circle, gave him the license he needed to accomplish his chemical escape. Long before he reached his fifteenth birthday, John's only illusion of peace and well-being was arrived at through alcohol or other drugs.

If we had realized John was using drugs, we'd have had the explanation for his increasing isolation, mood swings, hostility and irritability, money problems, why he didn't want us to know what he was doing.

Mike knew a great deal about what John was doing, but he kept it to himself. When Mike was twelve, John introduced him to the pleasures of pot smoking, exacting a pledge of silence. To some extent, Mike too began to withdraw from the family circle, not wanting to give away their secret.

Susan went back to college in the fall, glad to be out of John's way, still in the dark as to what he was doing. Even if she had known, Susie had done her own share of experimental pot smoking and beer drinking with her high school friends; she wouldn't have seen the harm in either.

Bob and I stopped talking *about* John. We tried to numb the pain by ignoring it. When we tried to talk *to* John, his standard response stopped the discussion cold.

"You're crazy! There's nothing wrong with me! If you'd get off my back, everything would be fine!"

We began to think we *might* be crazy and that John *might* be fine. He had wrapped his smoke screen securely around us. We were firmly locked into an emotional defense called *denial*—the refuge of every alcoholic and addict. There's nothing wrong with them, they say; the problem lies with everyone else. Families of substance abusers also become trapped in denial, which blocks out the fact that drugs and alcohol are the *real* problem:

"Oh, no, I'm sure it's not drugs. Lisa has emotional problems."

"Todd's just upset over his parents' divorce. It's been really hard on him. He'll get over it."

"Wayne is just a very sensitive person. I don't think he'd mess with drugs, and I know he doesn't drink."

"Donna can't seem to get over her grandmother's death. That's what is affecting her schoolwork and her attitude. She's a nice girl, too nice to mess around with drugs."

"Sure, Brett probably drinks a little beer, smokes a little

pot. All the kids do that. But the main problem is his learning disability."

"Matt hates his stepfather. That's why he's in trouble all the time—to get back at him."

"John is high-strung," we said at *our* house. "He is very sensitive, but he has far too much intelligence to use drugs. We just have to try harder to understand him."

The monstrous possibility that John might be an alcoholic and a drug addict at the age of fourteen was too painful to endure. We accepted his invisible, self-erected smoke screen as a part of our everyday life. It was a powerful defense against an unthinkable reality.

# CHAPTER THREE

# Out of the House, Out of Control, Out of Touch with Reality

_____ John's callousness toward Mike was painful to see. He rejected him, ridiculed him, fought with him, or ignored him, except when Mike had something that he wanted—such as money. Then he had no qualms about buttering Mike up. Once John got what he wanted, his promises were forgotten, the money was never repaid.

"Mom, I wish you'd do something about John," Mike complained. "He borrowed $10 from me, and he said he'd wash cars to pay it back, and now he won't get off his lazy butt! When are you and Dad gonna do anything about him?"

My response sounded feeble even to me. "Mike, you know how John is. You ought to know better than to lend him money."

"I know, but every time he talks me into it, and I forget. *This* time he promised he'd go fishing with me any time I wanted him to."

Mike resented John's exploitations and knew that much of what John was doing was wrong. Yet he wanted desperately to be accepted by his big brother. It was a hard spot to be in.

At the end of Christmas vacation, when Susan was leaving for school, her parting remarks gave us pause.

"I'm glad I could come home for Christmas. But I'm thankful to be going back to school, too."

Susie had always loved being at home with us. Bob was puzzled.

"Why, Susie?"

"This family is always in an uproar on account of John. I know I should love him because he's my brother, but sometimes I almost hate him. I hate the way he acts and the way he talks to you and Mom. I hate the way he treats Mike and me. He's turned into a real jerk."

"Don't be too hard on him, Susie. It's just a stage he's going through. He'll grow out of it."

"Well, all I know is when I'm at school I don't have to be worrying about him, and it feels good."

A letter from Susan soon afterward brought news.

Dear Mom and Dad,
    I have a chance to spend this summer in England, studying and traveling with a group from school. I really want to go. Would you consider it?

We gave our permission right away. We knew we would miss her, but we wanted her to have such opportunities.

I could surely identify with Susie's eagerness to get away. Things were so unhappy in our household, I often wondered whether I had the courage just to walk out and leave all the misery behind. This fantasy became very real to me. I imagined myself buying a one-way plane ticket to the West Coast, renting an apartment hundreds of miles away, going job hunting in a faraway city. I spent many evenings all alone in that nonexistent apartment, after days when the struggle seemed more than I could handle.

But whenever I thought of leaving, guilt reared its

intimidating head. I lacked the courage to go, knowing I wouldn't be able to stick it out on my own; my feelings for Bob and appreciation of my comfortable home kept me from running away. But the most powerful magnet was John. I believed it was my responsibility to keep John safe, to shield him from Bob's anger, to serve as his buffer against the consequences of his own self-destructive behavior.

I threw myself into my part-time job and tried to forget about things at home. But the telephone kept bringing me back to harsh reality—calls from the school; from other parents; from John himself, asking to leave school on various pretexts.

Bob found his own escape. He had many legitimate reasons to spend time away from the house: tennis, gardening, his practice, hospital and medical society meetings. He even started to train for a marathon—guaranteed to keep him on the road morning, noon, and night.

Getting John out of bed was usually a long-drawn-out ordeal, but on his fifteenth birthday he was up before 7:00 A.M.

"Have you forgotten today's my birthday?" he called out exuberantly. "Who's going with me to get my learner's permit?"

I looked at Bob; he looked at me. Neither of us was eager for John to start driving. In the end, Bob went with him. Once John had the permit in hand, it was the beginning of an extended nightmare. He was a terrible driver, erratic, nervous, unpredictable. By this time John was using speed in addition to alcohol and marijuana; we knew only that he alternated between lethargy and hyper-excitability. At night he complained he couldn't fall asleep; in the morning he was cross and sluggish.

He was so domineering about wanting to drive at every opportunity that it seemed easier just to give in. I was so uncomfortable with any expression of anger—even my own—that I suffered his tyranny in silence.

Bob conceded that John was a menace behind the wheel but counted on time and training to remedy things. After all, what American parent would stand in the way of a youngster who wanted to learn to drive? Confused and demoralized, neither of us could say no.

And so we all gritted our teeth and endured the near-misses, heart-stopping approaches to rear bumpers, full-throttle take-offs, and nerve-wracking turns. Attempts at instruction met with impatient scorn.

"I know what I'm doing! For crying out loud, why don't you give me a chance?"

Bob grew testier and testier when John was at the wheel, and Mike and I cowered in the back seat, praying we'd make it to our destination in one piece. John was absolutely in charge. Bob and I had completely lost touch with our parental backbone.

This was only one of many situations in which we found it impossible to distinguish the emotional turmoil of adolescence from a chemically disordered nervous system. It's a difficult puzzle to work out, because normal adolescence is accompanied by emotional ups and downs, sometimes of terrific magnitude. Not all such behavior is drug-induced. Such an episode now and again is probably no cause for serious concern.

*But if there is a progressive pattern* that includes isolation from the family, skipping school, lies or other forms of dishonesty, emotional instability, conflict with everyone in the household, loss of interest in extracurricular activities or hobbies, and trouble with authorities, it's a pretty reliable indication of substance abuse as the underlying cause. Failing grades and disappearance of money or other valuables are more clues, although we never experienced these. John's grades, in fact, were remarkably good—another red herring.

*Parents who do recognize these patterns must get help as soon as possible from knowledgeable substance-abuse professionals.* Delay will only make matters worse and could actually be fatal. *The sooner a family intervenes, the better the chances that a drug-abusing youngster can learn to live productively again.*

We needed help, but we didn't know how much. Nor did we know where to turn. We were still keeping our problems locked up in our own carefully constructed defenses of secrecy and guilt. We couldn't reveal our problem, for then everyone would know we had been parental failures—or so we believed.

In the hope of giving the family a pleasant evening now and then, Bob proposed going out to dinner. After each such event, I swore it would be the last. John invariably demanded to drive, and we always got into a conflict of some sort on the way to the restaurant. The meal progressed with everyone in sullen silence or with walking-on-eggs conversation, exactly like our family dinners at home. The boys could hardly wait to get out. Bob was grouchy and unpleasant. I was uncomfortable and unhappy. This was supposed to be a treat?

As one after another of John's friends reached their sixteenth birthdays, John's mobility increased even more. We were glad to let him go. If he stayed home, he fought with Mike or retreated to his room in a moody silence and turned up his stereo full blast. When Bob yelled at him to turn it down, John couldn't hear, and Bob would head for the stairs with blood in his eye. Then I would rush up the steps ahead of him to knock on the door and ask John to turn his stereo down before things got to the shouting-and-shoving stage. It was just easier and less stressful to let him go out.

And so we did, though we asked a lot of questions to give the impression we were still in control. John had evasive answers for every one. He knew he was in charge, and he made the most of it.

The university town nearby compounded our problems. The local taverns employed college students with a very relaxed atittude about I.D. cards. John and his sixteen-year-old friends had no difficulty buying drinks.

When I found a fake I.D. card in John's wallet, I cut the card up in pieces and threw it away. John simply ordered a new one from a comic book, the way he had obtained the first one. Nothing changed.

Suspecting that John was probably buying alcohol, I wondered whether he also could be using other drugs, and I began to search his room and clothing. I believed then, and I still believe that a parent is justified in searching the room of any youngster who is behaving strangely. I found several things I didn't understand, things that increased my suspicions and anxieties. But every such search left me feeling more confused and bewildered, guilty and afraid.

In the early stages, we were ignorant of the fact that rock concerts are notorious for drugs. Our boys were thirteen and fifteen when they first asked to attend a rock concert with friends. I didn't feel good about it, but after I got the Aw-Mom-you're-so-overprotective speech, I ignored my bad vibes and let them go. The following day, I found a package of rolling papers in John's jacket pocket. He said they belonged to a friend. I believed him! I also noticed something new on his bedside table.

"Son, I found these eyedrops in your room. Are you having trouble with your eyes?"

"What are you snooping around in my room for?" His stormy response silenced me. "They're eyedrops, normal eyedrops, the kind everybody uses. It's no big deal. My eyes were irritated from all the smoke at the concert."

Next, the little mesh aerator screens began to disappear from the faucets.

"Boys, do you know what's happened to the aerator on the kitchen sink?" No one knew.

A few weeks later: "Now the aerator's messed up in the downstairs bathroom. Do you guys know anything about it?" Not a clue.

In a month: "I just don't understand this. The aerator's gone out of my bathroom too. What's going on here?" John and Mike shrugged their shoulders.

This tiny mesh screen fits perfectly into the bowl of a marijuana pipe.

A surgical clamp disappeared from Bob's medical bag. Pot smokers use such a clamp as a roach clip—a holder that permits smoking a joint down to the last nub.

A bottle of tranquilizers disappeared from the medicine cabinet. We suspected the plumber!

I found what looked like a miniature tobacco pipe behind the books on John's shelf. He said it belonged to his friend Richard. I called Richard and asked him. He said it was John's. John said Richard was lying.

These things happened over a period of many months, far enough apart that we never put together the big picture. The previous mystery had often been forgotten by the time the next one cropped up. But all the signs were there. It was like the pictures in children's magazines—the ones in which you find the Indian hidden in the tree branches, or the hammer among the lily pads.

We could make no sense of our picture, because we were looking at the wrong things. John did so many of the things he should have been doing. He went to church with us regularly, participated in confirmation class, took part in the youth group, and was a faithful acolyte. He made the school honor roll and was elected vice-president of his class. He joined the yearbook staff. Occasionally he did go fishing or hunting with Mike. None of these things fit our imagined profile of an addict.

When hunting season rolled around, John and Mike went into the woods behind our house one Saturday to try for squirrels. But we didn't hear much shooting, and when the boys came in, they were silly and giggling, their eyes fiery red.

"Boys, what's wrong with your eyes? They look funny."

They found my question hilarious.

"Nothing's wrong," they laughed in a goofy, unfocused way. "Nothing's wrong. Not a thing."

Was I going crazy? Something *was* wrong. The boys just weren't behaving normally. They flopped down on the floor in front of the television, looking spaced-out and dreamy.

I went up to my room and closed the door, feeling sad, disturbed, shut out by these teenage louts. I lay on my bed and tried to figure out what was amiss, but I could make no sense of it. Instead, I thought about guns.

Guns had always been a source of concern for me. We lived in a rural area just outside town; the neighboring farm boys all had guns and regularly hunted birds, rabbits, and squirrels. I had been opposed to giving the youngsters guns, but Bob saw it differently.

"Honey, boys just naturally want to fool with guns. I'm teaching them the safe way to handle firearms, since they're going to do it anyway." Bob's explanations did make a certain kind of sense. He joined a rod-and-gun club, where the boys could shoot skeet, and enrolled them in a gun-safety course.

My doubts hung on. "Maybe it's silly, but I still just don't like the idea of having guns around. I worry about the boys getting hurt or hurting somebody else."

John and Mike always had their stock answer ready: "Aw, Mom, you're so *overprotective!*"

After being told that several hundred times, I had started to believe it, so I finally gave up and left the matter of the guns to Bob.

One weekend, Bob was working in the garage while John was in his room behind that closed door, the stereo blaring. John came downstairs for a snack, and at that moment, Bob came into the kitchen.

"John, you were supposed to wash the car today. You haven't done it."

"I'll do it after a while."

"I want it done now. Go ahead and get busy."

"I'll do it when I get ready," John mumbled sullenly.

Finally Bob blew his cool. "Dammit, John, I want it done *now!*"

John's response was equally explosive. "You go to hell!"

He glared hatefully at Bob, then stormed out of the kitchen and up to his room. In moments he was back, wearing his shell vest and carrying his double-barreled shotgun. He paused in the kitchen long enough to chamber two shells.

I was horrified. "John! Stop! What are you doing?"

"None of your damn business," muttered John as he elbowed past me out the door and headed for the woods.

"Bob, you've got to stop him! He shouldn't have the gun when he's in that frame of mind!"

"I'm afraid to try. The way he looked, I don't think he'd hesitate to turn that gun on either of us."

It was true. The look of cold rage that John had directed at us said unmistakably that he was not to be interfered with. Bob and I stood helplessly, waiting. In moments, the shooting began. John was firing as fast as he could reload—first one barrel, then the second—a moment of quiet, then two more explosions, and two more, and two more, on and on. We didn't know whether he was shooting into the air, at trees, or gathering his nerve to shoot himself. It was a blood-chilling wait.

At last he ran out of ammunition and came back to the house, sullen, silent, his rage spent for the moment. No one said a word. We were afraid to speak. And John retreated once more behind that closed door.

On Monday after the boys left for school, Bob gathered up all the guns and carried them to a friend's for safekeeping.

We lived constantly thereafter with the fear that John, enraged or despairing, might impulsively take his own life. In one of his bouts of depression, he expressed that very fear.

"Mom, sometimes I'm afraid I might kill myself."

Horrible words, unthinkable possibility—I turned it aside!

"Son, you mustn't even think such a thing, much less talk about it. Too many people care about you."

John very rarely shared his deepest feelings with others; now he had opened the smallest crack to let someone else participate in his torment. Not knowing how to respond, I suppressed it entirely, which is a very risky thing to do.

Youngsters who express thoughts of suicide often go on to carry out the final deed, particularly if drug or alcohol abuse has made a mess of their lives. Of every ten adolescent suicides, the bodies of at least seven contain significant amounts of alcohol or other drugs, and teenage males are four times more likely to commit suicide than their female counterparts. John could easily have killed himself on any of a number of occasions.

When his sixteenth birthday came around, he was champing at the bit to apply for his driver's license. We had misgivings, but we lacked the guts to tell him he wasn't ready. We hoped the privilege of a license would help him live up to the responsibility. It didn't work out that way.

John flunked his first driving test outright. The examiner told him to practice signaling and turning and come back in a week. Bob took John over the prescribed test course several times to make sure he could negotiate it. The second time, the examiner was still doubtful, but eventually he signed the form and told John he had passed.

A gleeful John began to take our car out on his own. Within a week, he zoomed out of a filling station into the path of a pickup truck. Incredibly, the investigating officer didn't charge John. We told him he'd have to pay for the damages. Nevertheless, the accident was reported to our insurance company and our premium skyrocketed.

With a big car-repair bill to pay, John got busy and found a job in a fast-food place. He was quite pleased with himself. Working after school and evenings, once again he was earning good money and made regular payments to the body shop. But he still had trouble with his checkbook, and our inquiries into his finances were met with hostility, just as before.

On the rare occasions now when John was home, he was chronically irritable and unpleasant.

"I'm getting sick of this," Bob complained. "We hardly ever see him, and when we do, every time one of us speaks to him, either he says nothing or comes back with some smart-aleck answer."

I grasped at every consolation. "At least he has a job."

But teenagers who have part-time jobs are more likely to be involved with drugs. They have more money, freedom, and mobility, and they usually are more interested in buying cars than in applying themselves to their studies. Their parents have much less influence and contact with them than before, and John was no exception. Once he got the body-shop bill paid off, he bought himself an old secondhand car and used both the car and his earnings for his own purposes.

His next wreck occurred on a weekend. A boy whose parents were out of town threw a big party. High on pot and beer, John backed into the car of another youngster, who was in the same shape. John's car wasn't hurt, but neither boy wanted his folks to know, so they made a quiet settlement on the side. John agreed to pay for the damages and did not report the incident to us. Whatever the other youngster may have told his folks, the truth escaped us at the time.

But a passing policeman saw the accident, stopped to investigate, and filed a report. Our insurance company received this news about the time I was trying to help John straighten out his checkbook again and came across a check made out to cash for $184, endorsed by the other boy. John was slower than usual in coming up with a convincing alibi and finally confessed that it was a payment for collision repairs. Our insurance premium soared again.

The third wreck came during the early-morning rush hour. John was driving to school, enjoying his first joint of the day. When the driver in front of him braked for a traffic light, John failed to stop in time. Again, the other driver was a teenager who didn't want to report the accident to her father's insurance company, and John agreed to take care of the damages. In the course of that one year, he shelled out $1,800 for car repairs.

Somehow we convinced ourselves that three wrecks in a year's time did not constitute a terribly abnormal situation! After all, insurance companies expect teenage boys to have more wrecks than anybody else. It even comforted us to hear that other kids had accidents too!

John began to stay out later and later on weekends, but he always had a first-rate excuse: a friend's car had stalled, a girl needed a ride home, a paycheck had to be picked up before closing. Such good excuses! John was a creative and spontaneous liar. And we believed him because we wanted to.

The first night he stayed out past 2:00 A.M., I panicked. Bob had turned in early. In an agony of indecision and worry, I finally mustered the nerve to call the parents of one of John's friends.

I heard a very grouchy male voice. "Hello!"

It was hard to sound casual at 3:00 in the morning, but I gave it a try.

"This is John's mother. I'm a little worried because John hasn't come in tonight. Is Chris home yet? I thought he might have some idea where John could be."

"Hold on, I'll ask him." I heard him say, "Go get Chris up. It's John's mom. She wants to know where John is." I held on, waiting.

"Chris came in at 12:30. He says the last he saw of John, he was with Brett, down on Fifth Street."

I went through the same process with Brett and his folks, and with David and his parents. Everyone was superficially polite; their youngsters had long been home in bed. Nobody knew where John was. I thanked each in turn and hung up, tears pouring down my checks. Paralyzed by anxiety, I couldn't even bring myself to wake Bob. I suffered in silence and alone, though the tightness in my throat seemed nearly to choke me.

At 3:45 A.M., John finally rolled in, knee-walking drunk. I tried to talk to him, but his only response was a muttered, "Shut up, bitch!"

Sick in my soul, I watched him stagger upstairs to bed. Rather than disturb Bob with a situation he could do nothing about, I nursed my misery alone until daylight. John would soon be seventeen, after all. And all teenagers are going to experiment with alcohol—aren't they? I lay awake, my pillow wet with tears.

John and I were not popular after that. The parents I had disturbed at 3:00 A.M. laid down the law to their kids—give John a wide berth. Bob and I told ourselves that John's friends were a bad influence on him. The truth was that John was the bad influence. Most of the other kids fooled around with beer and pot, but their lives were never out of control. John's life had been out of control since he was thirteen.

John was massively repentant the next morning. Bob hadn't the heart to lecture him when he saw how hungover he was. John brought the subject up himself.

"Mom, Dad, I want you to know I realize what a stupid

thing I did last night. I'm really sorry. I feel rotten about it. I don't blame you for anything you decide to do to me."

John couldn't say the word *drunk;* neither could we. Bob was moved by his contrition.

"Well, son, I'm relieved to hear you feel that way about it. It *was* stupid. I certainly can't let you continue to drive after such an irresponsible performance. Your mother and I will talk it over, but I think you'd better count on being grounded for at least a month."

"I don't blame you, Dad," said thoroughly penitent John. "I'm sure I deserve it."

When Bob and I left for church, John dragged himself back upstairs to bed, looking so miserable I was sure there'd be no repeat performance. But no matter how much John believed in his own promises, or how much Bob and I wanted to believe in them, *John could not help himself.* He had lost the power of choice. And it happened again, and then again.

The scene was always the same. John went out. Bob went to bed. I waited up, pacing the floor. John came in long past his curfew, often with slurred speech, red eyes, and unsteady gait. I assumed he had been drinking, but I didn't know how to deal with intoxication, nor could I confirm the use of other drugs. If I confronted him, he either cursed or stared me down with silent contempt.

I always waited until the next day to tell Bob what had happened, tailoring the story to protect John. Any conflict between the two contained the potential for uncontrollable violence. I believed I had to shield John from Bob and Bob from his own anger.

I was making myself responsible for everybody's actions—a terribly sick thing to do. I was the operator at our family's emotional switchboard, receiving all messages and compelled to take action on each and every one.

The lines all stayed so busy, I had no time to think there might just be some personal calls for me that weren't getting through. *When a family is struggling with addiction, everybody in that family begins to behave in sick ways.*

Yet when we clamped down on John, grounded him except for school or work, took away his driving privileges, or required extra chores around the house, he was totally submissive. He knew his behavior was out of line. He really wanted and tried to do better. It was simply beyond his power to stay sober or drug-free for more than a few days at a time. And it was beyond our power to recognize that fact.

Through it all, Mike stayed as far out of the line of fire as possible. When he heard a family conflict warming up, he headed outdoors to shoot a few baskets or turned up the volume on "Gilligan's Island." He knew a lot he wasn't telling—that John stole a bottle of vodka out of our liquor cabinet, drank most of it at a football game, and got in a fistfight that had to be broken up by security guards; that while Bob and I were out at a dinner party and John came in drunk, vomited all over the bathroom, and passed out, Mike had helped him clean up the mess. Mike kept these secrets for what seemed to him admirable motives—self-protection and loyalty. The only piece of the puzzle he lacked was the fact that John was killing himself.

An addict? A drunk? He was only sixteen! But John *was* addicted—to both alcohol and other drugs. He had no control over either. Whenever he used them, they took over completely. He never knew whether he could drink one beer and stop, or go on to twenty and pass out. He never knew whether he could share a joint and call it quits, or smoke three more and swallow a handful of pills besides. No one else could see what was happening to John, and John himself couldn't see it.

Our pastor was young, bright, thoughtful, and caring, a good friend to the family, so I sought him out for counseling. I wanted him to tell me how to make John behave and how to deal with Mike. This he could not do. He could only encourage me to look at my own life, ask myself why the same kinds of things happened again and again, take better care of myself emotionally, and open up my awareness. The man had gone through college and seminary in the chaotic 1960s, when pot was a whole generation's drug, one he had used himself. He thought it harmless, totally unaware of the havoc that mind-altering chemicals can cause in a family. He was caught up in denial, right along with the rest of us.

"All kids experiment with pot and beer," he reassured me, echoing words we were to hear from many others. "Be patient. They'll both grow up eventually." And so a potential avenue of help failed us, through no one's fault.

Clergy are often the first to be approached by suffering family members of addicts. Pastors desperately need to know how to recognize the chaos created by chemicals for what it is, and they must be taught how to intervene in the addiction process. Fortunately, many ministers, led by such pioneers as Joseph Kellermann, Vernon Johnson, and Stephen Apthorp, are now learning about the disease of addiction and referring tormented families to specialized help. But many still lack this all-important knowledge.

The next crisis came when John's boss accused him of taking money out of the cash register. John was indignant.

"You can forget about firing me," he said, flinging down his apron. "I quit!"

He walked out and brought his tale of injustice home. Taken in by John's declaration of innocence, Bob went with him to the employment office to file a complaint. The employment people told John his boss could fire him for any reason he chose, and Bob reluctantly suggested that John drop the matter. Had he persisted, we ultimately would have been embarrassed, for John *had* taken the money—a good deal of it—although his boss chose not to press charges.

John loafed around at home for a couple of months, feeling the pinch financially. Then, tired of being strapped for cash, he hustled up a new job as busboy. The money was good when the tips were generous.

We learned later that food-service jobs are notorious for availability of drugs. John never looked for any other kind of work—another clue for parents when a teenager's behavior raises suspicions about substance abuse. Does he or she work in a pizza place, steakhouse, or bar? Of course, not every such place is a haven for otherwise unemployable drunks and druggies, but many are. And even if the place happens to be free of other drugs, an alcoholic waitress or busboy can always cop a buzz by finishing up the dregs of customers' drinks.

One afternoon I came home from work earlier than usual to find John entertaining a visitor. A burly, bearded guy in the standard black-leather motorcycle rig was making himself comfortable on my living-room sofa.

"Mom, this is Angelo. Angelo, this is my mom," said John nervously.

I acknowledged the introduction, question marks doing jumping jacks in my head. Who the deuce was Angelo, and what was this older man doing with my sixteen-year-old?

Obviously, I had come home sooner than expected.

Angelo was slick and smooth, but I sensed his discomfort in my presence, and he soon left. I felt as though something extremely nasty had slithered through the hall and out the door. I was strongly inclined to count the silverware.

"John, I need some answers here. Who is Angelo, and what does he want with you?"

"Chill out, Mom! You're so *suspicious*! He's the fry cook at the restaurant. Angelo's new in town. He doesn't know anybody. He just wants some friends."

I wasn't buying this. Thirty-year-old motorcycle buffs don't seek out teenage buddies unless there is something very, very unusual going on.

"I don't care how many friends he wants. I don't want that character hanging around here. That guy is bad news."

"Some Christian you are," John sneered. "Can't even be nice to a stranger in town. You call that Christian charity?"

For once I held my ground. "John, no! I don't want him around here *ever*."

So after that John found other ways to see Angelo. He never brought him home again. Angelo was a drug dealer, and John was one of his first local customers. My vibes were right on target. I just lacked the proof.

Springtime came—always a bad time for families of substance-abusing kids. A car, a couple of six-packs, and a bag of grass can add up to trouble. The Saturday night John and three friends chipped in for several six-packs and a "dime" bag—$10 worth—of pot, they made the mistake of consuming them in a parking lot two blocks from the police station. The patrolman who arrested them just strolled over and led the quartet back to the jail on foot, by way of Main Street.

John was home that night by 9:30, but his early arrival gave no cause for rejoicing. He handed us a summons that required him to appear in Municipal Court to answer a charge of unlawful possession of beer and marijuana. We had our answer now—John *was* using drugs. Our worst fears were confirmed. And our juvenile-court days were over. John had graduated to the big boys' league. Bob and I weren't even surprised. By then we were chronically numb.

"Son, are you guilty as charged?" Bob asked wearily.

"The damn blue pig—"

Bob cut him short. "You are not to refer to a policeman in that disrespectful way in this house. Get that straight."

"Yes sir," said John, subdued.

"Did you do what it says on this summons?"

"Well, yes, Dad, but we weren't hurting anybody."

"Son, how long can we go on like this?"

"Like what?" John was buying time, a favorite ploy.

Bob exploded. "You know what! All these weeks and months of trouble with the law, car wrecks, coming in late, insolence, rudeness, sullenness, thinking you can thumb your nose at the world and get away with it!"

John listened in silence.

"Son, what do you have to say for yourself?"

"I don't know, Dad." John looked confused. His bravado had evaporated. "I don't know anything to say. I guess I'm just a criminal."

"Go up to your room. We'll talk about this in the morning."

"Yes sir," said John. "Good night, Mom. I'm sorry, Dad. I love you."

Those last three words kept us hanging on. John never forgot how to say "I love you," and so we kept doggedly on, trying to save him.

Going to court with John was humiliating. Many of the lawyers in the courtroom knew Bob, as did the judge. We felt very strange as our boy lined up with the town drunks. We had refused to hire a lawyer; Bob spoke to the judge on John's behalf. If we had it to do again, we would go to court with him, but let John speak for himself. If we had let him deal with the consequences of his behavior, he might have learned something. We thought we were helping, but actually we were standing in the way of progress.

The judge too thought he was helping. He told John what a fine family he came from, how fortunate he was that his parents were willing to come to court to stand up with him, that he believed in his basic good character and felt sure he wouldn't make the same mistake again. He dismissed the charge, fined John court costs of $25, and told him to walk the straight and narrow in the future.

John spoke only two words during his second court appearance: "Yes sir."

Once more, Bob and I took the responsibility for assuring the world that our boy would behave. Back home, we exacted a penitent promise. John assured us he had really learned his lesson and that our worries were over: "I'm finished with dope once and for all."

John's arrest and trial had been just one more scrape for him to squirm out of, unreformed. Two days later, to celebrate, he called Angelo and bought the biggest bag of grass yet.

# CHAPTER FOUR

# *Seeing the Elephant*

_____ **W**hen John became a high school junior, there was still lots of trouble at home, particularly on weekends, but we had learned to endure unpleasant situations.

Midway through the year came word from school: One summer-school course would give John enough credits to graduate from high school a year early. Pulled out of his habitual indifference, John responded to this discovery with a surge of positive energy.

"I'm sick of high school anyway," he declared. "It sucks!" (He applied this offensive expression to nearly everything.) "I'd *love* to go to college a year early!"

"You'd better get busy then," said Bob. "Admissions directors are already picking people for next year."

"What do I have to do?"

"Decide what college you're interested in, write for application forms, and get your principal to send your grades and a letter of recommendation."

"No problem!" John declared confidently.

We watched this transformation with amazement, daring to hope that college might do for John what nothing else had. He hadn't cared this much about anything for three years! He wrote the necessary letters, looked up college catalogs, asked his principal to supply transcripts.

In spite of his worrisome behavior, John's grades were well above average. His SAT score was in the top 1 percent nationwide, denoting a National Merit Finalist. Knowing most parents would give an eyetooth for such a record, we were ashamed to complain about the not-so-admirable parts of his performance.

Susie got wind of John's prospects and launched a campaign for him to apply to Chambers College, her own school.

"John, I'm so excited to hear about your plans to start college early!" she wrote. "I've already been to see the director of admissions here at Chambers, and he says your chances of getting in are good. Go ahead and mail your application as soon as you can. They'll look favorably on you, knowing you have a sister who's done well here."

Susan said nothing to the admissions director about John's problems at home. She too was trusting that college would fix everything.

The subsequent flurry of activity was a great morale booster for our family. Mike thought about how nice it would be to have John out of the house. Bob and I thought about Friday and Saturday nights of peaceful sleep, our house quiet again, no heavy-metal rock constantly blaring. And John voiced his feelings at the dinner table.

"It'll really be *cool* to go to college! I can do anything I want, and nobody will be there to say, 'John, I wish you wouldn't do that' or 'John, be in on time' or 'John, clean up your room.' No more hassles! I can hardly wait."

We other three exchanged glances. We too could hardly wait.

John's admission interview at Chambers went well and

prospects looked hopeful. Susie took him to class with her; he liked it, especially when the professors called him "Mr. White."

So John was accepted in college at age seventeen. A new day appeared to be dawning for our family. John had something he could commit to, and our hopes soared in spite of the caution we'd learned from previous disappointments. Susie couldn't stop talking about how glad she was that John was coming to Chambers. Focusing on her pride in her "little" brother and her love for him, she forgot how unpleasant his behavior could be.

We were putting our hopes into something that had already failed us once—the geographic cure. Boarding school had not solved John's problems, and basically, nothing had changed.

At summer's end, we took a family vacation in a rented cottage at the seashore—a good opportunity to pull things back together. The vacation started off happily enough. The boys got along unusually well together. They fished and surfed and goofed around on the beach with Susie. Bob and I lazed and read, swam, walked the beach, and enjoyed just sitting on the porch. We had more pleasant things to talk about than we'd had in a long time. Life was taking a positive and happy turn. With everybody in such a cheerful frame of mind, I didn't even mind cooking three squares a day for five big appetites.

Halfway through the second week, after a perfect day, John and Mike failed to appear when I called everyone to dinner. We waited at the table, and when they still hadn't come downstairs, I went up and opened the door of their room without knocking—something I ordinarily never did.

"Did you boys hear me calling you to dinner?"

Mike, lounging on the far bed, looked up warily from

his comic book. John, cross-legged on the near bed, looked up uneasily too, as well he might, because in front of him was the upside-down lid of the toilet tank, heaped full of marijuana.

I could not have been more shocked if I'd found him cuddling a boa constrictor. He'd been picking out the seeds and putting them in a spice tin. My mind shut down; my emotions took over.

"What the hell do you think you're doing?" I blurted. On blind impulse, I snatched up the tank lid, carried it to the bathroom, swept the marijuana into the toilet, and flushed it away, all in a matter of seconds.

The boys were stunned. Mike stood up, silent and fearful as he backed away from the coming fury. John sprang to his feet. A grown man in size, he was a fearsome presence, his jaw set, his face contorted with hatred.

"You goddam bitch, that's $70 worth of pot you just wasted!" He loomed menacingly above me. "I paid for it with my own money! It was mine!" At the brink of losing control, he drew back his fist. "Goddammit, I feel like killing you, you—"

My instinct for self-preservation finally revived. I grabbed the spice tin and fled, the door banging noisily against the wall. Bob and Susie heard the commotion as I clattered down the stairs in fear of my life, an enraged John hard on my heels. I made it to the foot of the stairs and dodged out of his path. As Bob moved to grab him, I reacted violently.

"Let him go!"

Bob backed off, realizing it was dangerous to interfere. John flung the two of us roughly aside, pushed past Susie, and plunged through the screen door toward the beach. He was in the grip of the black fury so typical of his behavior in those dark days.

Bob put his arms around me. I was trembling uncontrollably. "Honey, what happened?"

"Better see where he goes." I didn't know what John might do next. We stood watching at the screen door as he charged angrily between the dunes and took off down the beach away from the house.

Susan grasped my hand tightly in her ice-cold one. "Mama, what is it?"

"Now tell me what this is all about." Bob led me to the sofa. I took a deep breath to steady myself and told the story.

"Thank God he didn't hurt you," Bob said.

"Mama, you took a *big* risk," said Susie. "You're lucky he didn't do something really crazy."

"Well," said Bob dispiritedly, "I guess it's pretty obvious John hasn't given up smoking pot after all. I had hoped that problem was under control."

"How much did he have?" asked Susie.

"I don't know. He said it was $70 worth. Here's the box with the seeds."

Susie poured the seeds into her palm. There was half a handful. They looked like tiny peppercorns.

"He must have had an awful lot to begin with, probably two or three ounces at least. That's a lot of pot. He's either smoking huge amounts himself, or he's selling it."

We sat there in troubled silence.

In a few minutes Mike came downstairs and went into the dining room without saying a word. Our dinner had grown cold on the table, but he sat down and began to pile food on his plate. His style in those days was to remove himself completely from the violent conflicts that cropped up with frightening regularity in our household.

Finally Susan spoke, her voice breaking. "I'm so scared

about John! This is *serious*! Can't you do something about him?"

Bob and I had no answers. For nearly four years we had struggled, clinging to our belief that John was having a rough adolescence and eventually would outgrow his problems. We expected difficulties with teenagers. To a lesser degree, we were having problems with Michael. Boys will be boys, we kept telling ourselves.

Susan persisted. "I'm serious, Daddy. I think John's been doing a whole lot more drugs than you and Mama know. I love John, and if you let him keep on like this, something terrible is going to happen!" Her pent-up tears poured forth at last.

We could no longer escape the knowledge that John was in deep trouble; we were barely beginning to face up to the nightmare reality that his problems might be centered on drugs. What to do about it was another matter.

"I know you're right, Susie," said Bob. "Mom and I will talk things over and come to some kind of decision about what to do. We certainly can't do anything right this minute. Let's try to forget it for now and not let it ruin our whole vacation. Okay?"

"Okay," said Susie.

I was still slumped in dejection on the sofa, but Bob wanted things to return to normal. He gave me a hand up.

"Come on in the dining room, honey. Susie and I can warm up the supper. Let's enjoy our meal. We don't have to let this business with John ruin *everything*."

Mike still sat, cleaning his plate in silence. Bob confronted him.

"Michael, why didn't you tell us John had all that dope?"

Mike shrugged indifferently. "I didn't feel like getting killed."

My head was swimming; I felt queasy. "Bob, I don't think I can eat right now. You and Susie go ahead, but I need some time to myself. I think I'll walk down to the dock before the sun goes down."

"Okay, honey, if you're sure you'll be all right," said Bob. "Susie, how about you?"

"I'm not hungry either, Daddy, but I'll keep you company." The two of them had thrown off the sudden gloom brought on by John's behavior. But for me, the clouds wouldn't go away.

As I made my way down the boardwalk, all my perceptions were dulled. I could barely think; my vision was blurred, and I couldn't hear well. My heart was pounding, and there seemed to be a buzzing inside my head.

Frightened and sad, I was homing toward my favorite place of serenity, the tidal marsh. The marsh is a refuge I often seek on our vacations when the noise of children and radios and motorbikes seems overwhelming—a changeless place where I can get back in touch with deeper currents.

The last rays of the sun were shedding a quiet peace over the watery expanse of sawgrass. I hoped none of the neighbors would be on the dock, for I wanted desperately to be alone. Not knowing what else to do for comfort, I began to pray as I walked along. *God help me,* I said inwardly again and again.

I continued to repeat the words as I sat on the dock. Why was this happening to me? What had I done to deserve it? Heartbroken, I mourned the loss of my loving son. I feared and even hated the violent, unpredictable stranger who had taken his place.

Finally my breathing became more steady. The buzzing noise began to die away. I heard a splash as a mullet jumped in the channel. The pounding of my heart slowed. I continued to grieve, but my panic and despair were fading. The question persisted—*Why me?*

No answer came. At last, sitting there in the twilight, I realized my world wasn't going to end just yet. As I watched the snowy egrets planing homeward across the marsh in the sunset's afterglow, a soothing calm came over me. My courage and inner strength were timidly returning. I didn't know what lay ahead, but for the moment, the sense of peace that enveloped me in the gathering darkness was enough.

At last I walked back to the cottage. Bob and the two kids had finished supper and cleaned up the kitchen. The atmosphere was noticeably lighter. John hadn't come back.

"Feel better, Mom?" Susie asked.

"Much."

"Good!" Susie knew Bob and I needed time alone to talk. "Mike, how would you like to walk with me up to the pier?"

"Okay, sure. Can I take my fishing stuff?"

"Fine with me. We'll both fish, if you want to."

After they had gone, Bob brought two cups of coffee into the living room and sat down. The house was very still. "Well, where do we go from here?"

"You know as much as I do."

"While you were down at the dock, I came up with a plan," he said. "See what you think of this. For the next month, until John leaves for college, I say we keep him absolutely grounded. We'll take away his use of the car. We won't let him leave the house unless one or the other of us goes along. We won't allow his friends to visit him. It's the only way we can be sure he doesn't get hold of any more dope before he leaves for school. I think we may just be able to help him straighten himself out."

Bob's plan was something to hold on to, at least. In my stunned and wounded state, I could think of nothing better.

"It's worth a try. I don't know what else to do."

We agreed not to tell John about it until we were home, to avoid adding any more fuel to an already volatile situation. Bob and I comforted each other as best we could that night, hoping we had solved our problem, telling ourselves we could work things out. Surely it was just a matter of tightening control and talking John around to a rational way of life.

When he finally came back, he barged into the living room like a boiling thunderhead and launched into an abusive monologue.

"Mom, you're lucky you didn't get hurt." His voice was nastily self-righteous. "I felt like killing you. I still do."

I listened in silence.

"You may think you're so *holy* and *good*, but the truth is, you're a criminal, a common thief. You stole my pot from me, just *stole* it." His voice grew louder, and his rage continued to build. "Where do you get off, thinking you're in charge of my life, anyway? And Dad's just as bad as you are. He takes up for you in everything. He's against me too, just like you. Why don't the two of you just get off my back? I can handle my life just fine, if you two goddam stinking hypocrites will ever get the hell out of it!"

We took John's profane tirade coolly, in the wake of our new resolve. He may have realized how wild he sounded or sensed a change in our attitude, for although he was sullen and scornful those last few days at the beach, he didn't leave, nor did he carry out any of his threats. We simply tried to ignore his rudeness, his sullenness and hostility. Placing complete reliance upon Bob's plan, we felt we were beginning to move forward.

We also believed, naively, that a month of living clean was all John needed to get straightened out. How ignorant we were about his disease—so ignorant we didn't even know it *was* a disease. We were barely beginning to get a look at our particular monster.

We would later hear other families talk about drug abuse as "the elephant in the living room." Everyone knows the elephant is there, but everyone ignores it. There had been a pachyderm in our parlor for several years now. We had caught glimpses of trunk or tail but pretended we hadn't. People outside the family had seen parts of our elephant, too, but no one had identified it for what it was. Now, undeniably, we had seen the whole enormous beast at close range—its trunk, tail, ears, body, and all four feet. John's elephant could on longer be ignored.

Yet we still did not know how to take hold of the elephant's rope to lead it away. We had felt its leathery hide and heard it trumpeting full blast, but in our ignorance, we tiptoed around the beast for nearly three more years. Chemical dependency, addiction, substance abuse—whatever we call it today—we were then only beginning to appreciate it for what it is.

No matter how we tried to make the rest of our vacation pleasant, we were left feeling wretched, obsessed with John and his problem. It colored everything a dull gray, even on the brightest days. The sun must have sparkled on the sea every day, but Bob and I couldn't see it. Susan tried to keep things cheerful, but it was an uphill battle. Mike and John spent the remaining days sitting glumly on their surfboards; at night they read comic books or fished on the pier. Nobody had any fun.

When we were home at last, the essentials of our plan fell into place. John accepted his house arrest more readily than we'd expected. Could it be that he really wanted to break free of his habit, grateful for our attempt to help him? He came to meals and watched television peaceably with the family. He stopped shutting himself up in his room. He listened to his music far less than before. He played Scrabble and went to movies with the rest of us. It was heartening to see Susan, John, and Mike enjoy one another's company, rather than avoid one another or squabble.

We saw more of John in that month than we had in the past couple of years, and he was fun to be with again. He helped with the dishes, carried out the trash, even got a haircut—whatever we asked him to do—in a docile and agreeable way. All of us were able to love John again—even to *like* him—and he seemed to like us again too. Believing our family affection and togetherness could pull John out of his hole, we welcomed him back and laughed and joked and were happy together. It felt like coming home, for as long as it lasted.

Yet even though big, husky John remained drug-free for the whole month, he seemed curiously fragile. Shaky, he cried at the least provocation. He sometimes worked himself into a state of manic excitement; at other times he was almost suicidally depressed. Once he accidentally cut his finger, quite superficially, and passed out. He had to leave a church service when he felt he might faint. I assumed he was suffering symptoms of withdrawal from his drug of choice—pot—which nearly any teenager will tell you glibly is not addictive. John's behavior belied that myth. He was chemically dependent, and had been for at least three years. We had never heard of the disease of chemical dependency.

John and I talked a lot during that drug-free month. One day we carried a picnic lunch to the nearby mountains. With a soft rain falling, we walked in the woods, admired the wildflowers, took in all the refreshing sights and smells of nature. John seemed to have shed his habitual bravado, his supercool facade. That day he seemed unusually open, younger than seventeen. In some ways he appeared vulnerable and sad as we ate our sandwiches beneath a tree among the ferns and trillium.

Feeling my way carefully into an opportunity, I told him gently that he appeared to have become dependent on pot, that his dad and I hoped this month of staying clean before he started college was the chance he needed to give it up once and for all. John appeared to be listening as I described what I thought pot was doing to him. I believed he wanted to break free, and perhaps he did.

We thought will power was all John needed to give up drugs. How little we understood the disease! Our rigid control during that month was the only thing that kept him abstinent. Had alcohol or pot been within reach, he could not have left them alone, for John was an addict.

He knew of no other way to feel good. He dealt with pain—emotional or physical—by blocking it out with alcohol or other drugs. Whenever chemicals were available, he would again choose this self-induced anesthesia.

John left for college at last. Our hopes were high. Chambers was a small liberal-arts college, noted for academic excellence and community spirit. We hoped with all our hearts that John would be stimulated intellectually, make worthy friends, be transformed from an aimless and hostile boy into a directed, outgoing, dynamic young man. We expected college to do all that!

But although a new world of possibilities was available at Chambers, by the time John enrolled there, he was already out of reach, walled off in an invisible prison. The changes we had seen were not to be lasting. We were not yet out of the woods. The way ahead was tortuous and long, and we would need a better map than the one we had if John were to have a chance to make it through.

# CHAPTER FIVE

# Dungeons, Dragons, and the Dead

_____John had to take a chemistry placement test during the first week of school.

On the way to the exam, a studious looking fellow freshman asked, "Are you a chemistry buff too?"

"No way, man!" was John's emphatic reply. "I'm just waiting for the party to start!"

Delighted with his own wit, John told us this story the first time we phoned him. There was a not-so-funny undertone to his quip, for there he was setting the scene for his college career.

Fraternity rush was one of the first events of the school year. John threw himself into it feverishly, and Susan was soon getting feedback from her friends:

"Say, Susie, your brother's a wild man!"

"Your little brother really enjoyed the rush party last night—he was drunk as a skunk by 8:00!"

She didn't pass these upsetting remarks along to us, but the next time she saw John, she told him what she was hearing and cautioned him about his behavior.

"Listen, John, if you make a fool of yourself during rush, you probably won't get a pledge bid at all."

"*You* listen, Susie! The main reason I came here was to get everybody off my back at home," John said testily. "My social life is *my* business. Your social life is yours. I'm not bugging you, so you can stop bugging me!"

After that, Susan suffered in silence. Her embarrassment was intensified when John was blackballed by the only fraternity he had the faintest hope of being invited to join. This house had a double-barreled campus reputation: high IQs and lots of drugs. Their parties were wild, but John's behavior went even beyond their far-out limits.

We waited for letters from John, but we had no contact with him unless we called. He was letting us know loud and clear that he wanted to be left alone. When we speculated about how he was faring, Bob only said, "I hope the boy's decided once and for all to leave the drugs alone." The unhappy expression on his face told me how shaky that hope really was.

For the first grading period, John pulled three Cs and two Ds. We were disappointed, to say the least.

"Are you doing your best, John?" I asked on the phone.

"I'm doing as well as I intend to do. I've set a perfectly respectable goal for myself—a solid C average. I'm not planning to study twenty-four hours a day like Susie does. I intend to have some *fun!*"

"Son, we're expecting more than that," Bob spoke from the other extension.

"Well, you'll probably be disappointed."

Parents' Weekend came around. Our visit with John was a disaster. The gentle, vulnerable youngster who had told us good-bye a few weeks earlier had vanished. The "old" John was back again—scornful, moody, rude. John knew nothing of the events planned for the visiting parents. He had bought no tickets to meals, sporting events, or the drama club play. He was reluctant to introduce us to any of his friends and accepted our offer of a steak dinner (washed down with a couple of beers) with a minimum of grace.

While Bob paid the bill for our meal I hung back long enough to ask John the all-important question:

"Son, have you stuck to your resolve to stay away from drugs?"

He eyed me distastefully. "Why don't you shut up?"

"Shhh!" I laid a restraining hand on his arm. But John wouldn't be shushed.

"Quit shushing me, dammit! Why did you and Dad come down here, anyway? It was *your* idea to come. The school invited you. I didn't, and I didn't care whether you came to the stupid Parents' Weekend."

John's rejection hurt so deeply that I could think of nothing to reply. Unaware of what had been said, Bob drove us back to the campus in a tense silence. When we arrived at the dorm John promptly excused himself, saying he had to go up to his room for a few minutes.

My question had been answered beyond any doubt. When John was smoking dope regularly he was hostile and sullen. "Mellowing out" was something we had never experienced at our house. John's pot personality was back, in full bloom.

"Is anything wrong?" Bob asked me, as we waited on front campus for John.

"Well, are you enjoying Parents' Weekend? I'm certainly not."

"No, I'm not either. John's acted like a complete jackass."

"I'm glad you didn't hear what he said to me at the restaurant."

"What was it?"

"There's no need to go into it. Let's just say he's back to his old hateful, rude self."

"The little jerk! Do you know why?"

"I think I do, but there's no use talking about it any more. Suppose we just leave now and head for home. I can't see any point in staying. In fact I don't think I can *stand* to stay any longer."

"Fine with me. I'll be relieved to get out of here."

When John came down, much more self-possessed—he'd been gone long enough to smoke part of a joint—we told him of our change in plans.

"Okay. Sorry you can't stay. I'll be seeing you around Thanksgiving, I guess." He waved us casually out of the parking lot.

On the drive home I choked back tears of disappointment. I saw no point in burdening Bob with all the details. We were apparently powerless to exercise any further control over our boy.

Now, for the first time, I found it more comfortable just not to see John, not to know what he was doing, not even to hear from him. We stopped talking about him at home.

And things got worse between Bob and me. John's situation depressed us to the point that we had no energy left for our own relationship. I was angry with John, angry with Bob for distancing himself from the problem. But I couldn't recognize that anger; being angry went against everything I'd ever been taught—turn the other cheek, forgive seventy times seven. So that suppressed anger turned itself back upon me in the form of self-loathing and chronic depression.

The great effort I expended in numbing myself to our miserable situation bore other dark fruit as well. In steeling myself to ignore feelings of anger, disgust, contempt, and fear, I also sacrificed the power to experience joy, excitement, anticipation, desire.

My blood pressure went up, requiring medication. I started to have headaches. I gained weight steadily and had a constant pain in my abdomen. I was locked in with my feelings of guilt—I must have been a horrible mother to produce such an antisocial child. I resented Bob's lack of awareness, blind to the fact that I had fostered that attitude myself by shielding him from knowledge of John's misdeeds.

Bob began to experience insomnia, disabling bouts of esophageal spasm, and chronic nervous tension. He was haunted by fears for John's future: Was his son mentally ill? Or was he a sociopath, destined to waste his existence in conflict with the institutions of a decent society?

These negative messages that played in our heads every day were so powerful that we couldn't even share them with each other. Although we didn't speak of John, he was constantly in our thoughts. He might have moved out of the house, but his smoke screen was still very much with us. It made us physically ill, precluded normal feelings and relationships, clouded our homelife at every turn. John's disease had robbed us all of the joy of living.

At Thanksgiving John spent the shortest possible time at home. Our brief family holiday was a miserable rerun of the past, except that this time we ignored John's behavior and made no effort to control him.

Mike complained loudly. "You're on my case all the time! You won't let me stay out late, or have the car, or anything else. But John comes home, and you let him get away with murder!"

"John is two years older than you," we said. "He goes to college." We knew the explanation wasn't good enough, but we couldn't admit John was beyond our control.

We *could* maintain limited control over Mike, which fed his already considerable resentment.

Susie probably carried a bigger emotional burden than anyone else in the family that year. On campus, although she avoided John, her friends told her about his antics. She confided her worries only to her boyfriend Dave and roommate Lisa.

She too was locked in a kind of self-imposed isolation. Her senior year should have been her last light-hearted youthful fling; instead, it was permeated with sadness.

Before Christmas, she made a bid for help. Learning that one of the college deans was supposedly trained in drug counseling, she went to see him and disclosed her concern about her brother. Dean Smith seemed more than willing to help. He suggested that Bob and I come to Chambers to talk things over. We drove down on the last day before Christmas break.

The dean listened attentively as I recounted our struggles with John.

"In a nutshell, Dean Smith, John's gotten off to a bad start. We hoped he would seize the opportunity in college to make something of himself, but his schoolwork is bad, his attitude is all wrong, and from all indications, we think he must be smoking marijuana pretty heavily. We haven't found a way to stop it, but if the college will back us, maybe we can get somewhere."

"We certainly should be able to help you. That's what we're here for. After Susan came to see me, I checked around, and from all I can gather, your assessment of John is pretty much on target. What would you like us to do?"

Bob spoke up. "In a few months, John will be eighteen. We've made up our minds. We're through supporting him at that point unless he gets some help for himself. Does the college have a counseling service where he could be seen regularly?"

"Absolutely," said the dean. "We have several excellent clinical psychologists. I can arrange for John to see one of them on a regular basis."

I was dubious. "He'll try his best to get out of it. I know John. He'll worm his way out of every plan we put together unless it has some very sharp teeth in it."

"I'll supply the teeth," said Bob. "I'll tell him, here in Dean Smith's presence, that unless he sees the counselor faithfully, we're cutting him loose. Can you hold him to that, Dean Smith?"

"Yes indeed. I'll have John check with me once a week to let me know how he's doing."

We were satisfied. It seemed like a watertight plan. Dean Smith picked up the phone to call John in.

We had stumbled onto an extremely useful tool: *Conduct any critical confrontation in the presence of an influential and impartial third person.* Dean Smith could, if he chose, expel John; if necessary, he could hold that threat over John's head indefinitely. We were banking on the probability that John would control his anger in the dean's presence.

When John walked through the door and saw us, his surprise was evident.

"Thanks for coming in, John," said the dean. "Please have a seat. Your folks have come in today to discuss your situation with me. I believe they have some legitimate concerns. I'll let them tell you about it."

Bob took the lead, speaking firmly and with an air of decision. "Son, your mother and I are very disappointed in the way you've started out the year here. Your grades are not good. Your attitude toward us has been unpleasant, and you've embarrassed your sister by your behavior. We're convinced you're mixed up with marijuana again."

John said nothing, but stared grimly ahead.

My old compulsion to plead took over, as it had so many times before.

"Don't you see, John, that you'll never get anywhere as long as you keep on fooling with the stuff?"

John's scornful gaze passed right through me as though I hadn't spoken.

"Dean Smith has agreed to back us in a plan," Bob went on. "You'll be eighteen in a couple of months."

John turned his glare on his father. The intensity of his emotion showed in his glittering eyes and flushing cheeks.

"Son, unless you accept some help for your problem now, I'm sorry to say that your mother and I are prepared to cut you loose altogether at that point."

John listened stonily, a muscle flickering in his jaw.

Bob continued, "You'll have to support yourself, of course, but on the other hand, you can live any way you please, with no interference from us."

"Unless you do accept help, John," the dean put in, "the college will assume you're not willing to put forth the maximum effort. At that point, we'll require you to withdraw from school."

We waited for John's response. He sat in silence for a few moments, containing his anger by a visible effort.

"Well. It looks like you've got me backed into a corner."

"I wouldn't call it that," said Bob. "We see it as a choice. It's entirely up to you. Accept help and begin to make the most of school, or get out on your own."

"I don't think it's a choice," John said. "It's an ultimatum. You've obviously got me where you want me."

Dean Smith's tone was conciliatory, "We're all on the same team here, John—*your* team. Your folks want to help you, I want to help you, the college wants to help you. All you have to do is accept the help being offered."

John thought it over for several moments. "What do I have to do?"

"When you come back from the Christmas break, I'll have an appointment lined up with one of the school psychologists. You'll see that person on a regular basis and report to me once a week about your progress."

"What if I don't do it?"

"Well, if you don't live up to the agreement, I'll let your parents know, and you'll have to leave school. It's pretty simple."

"Okay," said John tersely. "I don't think I have any choice."

"I'm glad you see it that way," said the dean. "I really believe things will begin to get better for you. I certainly hope so."

"Can I go now?"

"Yes, that's all we need from you." Dean Smith stood up to see John out. "Thanks again for coming in. I'll be in touch with you later."

John nodded. As he turned curtly on his heel and walked out, he directed a backward glance at Bob and me: *I'll get you for this.*

For once, John's raw hostility did not intimidate me. I felt joyous and relieved, for a major milestone had been passed. We had seen John control himself in the presence of another person who could exercise power over his situation. Until then, we had thought he was uncontrollably unbalanced, an emotional "loose cannon" who had to be handled with kid gloves.

That day, John revealed himself as a superb manipulator of people. He realized that Bob and I had reached our bottom line, and he tailored his behavior accordingly. He gauged Dean Smith's power instantly. Because he wanted the Chambers College diploma, he modified his behavior rather than indulge in a violent outburst. For the first time, we realized that John was a consummate actor. How liberated we felt!

John and Susie came home the next day for the holidays. Things seemed better.

On the afternoon of Christmas Eve, Bob and I went to a neighborhood open house. When we came home, Susie was waiting in the living room, her eyes red.

"I'm sorry to tell you this," she said, "but I have to. A friend of Mike's came by this afternoon. I'd never seen this Lanny Green before, but I didn't like his attitude. In a few minutes Mike and John went out the back door with him. I wondered what they were up to, so I went out to check. The three of them were up in the garage loft, getting high.

"I sent the Green kid home. I told John and Mike I was telling, and they should stay in their rooms until you came home. They're still up there. They're furious with me."

Bob and I exchanged a familiar expression: *We've been here before*.

"How do you think we should handle this?" Bob asked me.

"Let's call the Greens and tell them we need to see them. Too bad it's Christmas Eve, but I think we'd better go over there and talk it over anyway."

"I guess that's the thing to do." Bob sounded old and very tired.

We barely knew the Greens. Socially prominent people,

they traveled in our little town's version of the jet set. Their impressive house was lavishly decorated for Christmas. It seemed terrible to bring our miserable story to them at such a time, but they were gracious and thanked us for coming. Mr. Green promised to have a talk with Lanny and get back to us.

When we drove home, we saw the Christmas tree lights shining through the front window. Susie had turned them on in an effort to cheer us. As far as I was concerned, the tree might as well have been shrouded in black. I felt completely drained. Even though we'd arranged for John to start counseling, I didn't believe we'd turned a corner at all. We were still bogged down in the same old struggle, still smothering behind our screen of smoke.

At church that night, the boys sat beside us in sullen silence. Susie held my hand. Bob's face was stoic, inexpressive. I found a little comfort in the brilliant poinsettias, the living flames of the candles, and the age-old words and music of Christmas. For those two hours, at least, it hurt just a little less.

Mr. Green phoned the next day. We were all the more disappointed when he gave us Lanny's version of events—that Mike had paid for half of a bag of pot if Lanny would buy it and split it with him. Lanny had delivered it on Christmas Eve as promised.

We confronted Mike. Under pressure, he confirmed Lanny's story. So now we had *two* drug users on our hands. We had no idea what to do about Mike, other than to ground him for the rest of the holidays along with John, lecture him sternly, and warn him to stay clear of Lanny, who had been warned to stay clear of Mike. We had no more trouble with Mike for the remainder of the vacation. Unlike John, he seemed well able to discipline himself.

Susan's boyfriend, Dave, came to visit after Christmas, bringing a thrilling surprise—an engagement ring— which he presented to Susan on New Year's Eve. Her joy was complete, for she had come to love Dave very much over the year they'd been dating. He was a fine young man, moving up in a promising career, and we could see that he and Susie were very much in love. We gave them our blessing and celebrated with an extra-special champagne dinner party. Their plans to marry after Susie's graduation brightened our family's otherwise gloomy horizon.

A few days after Susie and John returned to school, we phoned to check on John's counseling efforts. He had seen the counselor, he said, and she was "beautiful and nice." I had hoped for someone ugly and tough.

"Did you report to Dean Smith?"

"I went by his office, but he had gone to the West Coast. I'm supposed to go back later this week."

"When's your next appointment with the counselor?"

"Next week. She's seeing me once a week."

"Okay. Take care of yourself, son. We love you."

"Yeah. Later," said John.

The next week the story was the same—Dean Smith was away from campus much of the time, and John's counselor, Dr. Lannon, was "as nice as she could be."

After the third week's phone call, we began to fear our plan hadn't been as watertight as we'd hoped.

"Son, did you see Dr. Lannon this week?"

"Yeah. I saw her yesterday."

"What did you talk about? Are you making any progress?"

"She wanted to know a lot of stuff about my family, what I did in high school, how I like college. I told her a lot about you all." *I bet you did,* I said to myself.

"What does she say about your drug problems?"

"Oh, we haven't gotten to that yet. She has to get some background first."

"What does Dean Smith think about all this?"

"I haven't seen him yet. He won't be back from New York until Friday."

Subsequent reports were no more encouraging. John wouldn't bring up the question of his drug use unless we pressed him. Finally, he told us the counselor had asked if he wanted to stop using drugs; he had said no.

"In that case, I really can't help you," she told him. "You might as well stop coming until you do want to quit."

Dr. Lannon was probably right. *She* couldn't help him—but *someone else could have,* and she should have referred John to a competent substance-abuse professional. She also should have steered Bob and me to counseling or a self-help group such as Al-Anon or Families Anonymous. Her failure to do so, and Dean Smith's failure to follow through on our plan, cost us a great deal of time. When we realized the plan was failing, John's tuition for the rest of the year had already been paid. Outmaneuvered once again, we were right back at Square One.

That spring was a total blast for John. He went to every party within miles and kept open house in his room the rest of the time. When he wasn't partying, he spent hours playing a pothead version of Dungeons and Dragons. He didn't date, but hung around with other bright boys who were chronically stimulated or stupefied by chemicals, socially immature and lacking in self-esteem. They made up for that lack by a great show of being cool and behaved in a variety of outrageous ways to draw attention to themselves.

John became interested in the Grateful Dead, a rock band left over from the 1960s. Grateful Dead fans are called Deadheads, and many are into drugs. John wanted us to share his enthusiasm for the Dead; we were mystified as to the attraction. He began to collect Grateful Dead tapes and traveled far and wide to their concerts with his Deadhead friends.

John's first roommate finally moved out, fed up with the Dead-mania and drug-centered social life. Lance, another Deadhead, moved in, to John's delight. We never met Lance, but on the phone, he sounded like John's clone—resentful and uncommunicative. John never received the messages we left with Lance, or so he said.

The end of the school year found us at an impasse. John's grades were still poor, but not bad enough to expel him. Bob and I were torn between the desire to cut him loose altogether and the fear that, with no skills, he would turn to drug dealing and end up dead or in prison. He had the option of enlisting in the military, but if he went in and was then found to be a drug abuser, he would be dishonorably discharged.

So we protected John and prevented him from suffering the painful consequences of his behavior. We decided to let him go back to Chambers the next year, and our inconsistency sent some very confusing signals. We were telling him, in effect, *You can't make it out there on your own; therefore we're going to let you continue your drug-centered life.* We enabled him to stay sick, rather than taking the tough stance that would help him recover.

# CHAPTER SIX

# Wedding Bells and a Ride on the Tiger

_____ $S$usan and Dave set the date for their wedding—a month after Susan's graduation. We began to shop for a wedding dress and veil, and all the other things that go into weddings. We sought out florists, caterers, photographers, stationers. Susie and I conferred often by telephone and mailed back and forth swatches of material and clippings from magazines. It was a welcome change from worry about John.

During spring break, Dave came for several days to help wrap up the plans. The couple had already seen our pastor to reserve the date and begin their premarital counseling; now they met with the organist, selected the music, and bought their wedding rings. Orange blossoms were in the air!

Dave's affection for our family had always been obvious; it now seemed even greater. He demonstrated a fondness for John and Mike in spite of their struggles in growing up. The brothers were visibly pleased when he asked them to serve as groomsmen, and the three returned in boisterous good spirits from being measured for their cutaways.

After Dave left, Susan came to me.

"Mama, you know I love John and Mike, and Dave loves them too. We really want them in our wedding. But I can't help worrying that John might do something to mess it up. Will you talk to him?"

"Indeed I will. If he causes any trouble, he'll have me to answer to. Daddy and I want your wedding to be the happiest day of your life, honey. We'll do everything possible to make it so."

John slept until noon that day, as he did during most vacations. When he finally came downstairs, I was having lunch.

"Mom, how about fixing me some breakfast?"

"It's too late for breakfast. I'm having lunch."

"Then fix me some lunch."

"In a few minutes. I want to talk to you about something first."

"Yeah? What?"

"You know, John, Dave has done you and Mike an honor by asking you to be his groomsmen."

"Yeah, I know."

"There's more to it, John, than just looking cool and dressing up in fancy suits. Dave really needs your help to see that everything's taken care of. You have some responsibilities."

"Okay, Mom. Everything's cool," John said grouchily.

"And you have another part to play, too, as a member of our family. We'll be the hosts for Dave's friends and family, as well as our own. Daddy and I expect you boys to help us welcome everyone and see that they're pleasantly entertained. You have to take these responsibilities seriously. If you'd rather not be bothered, let us know right now, and tell Dave you're dropping out of the wedding."

"What do you think I am, an idiot? If Dave wants me in the wedding, I'll *be* in the wedding."

"Maybe I'm not making myself clear, John. Every time there's a big occasion, a holiday or something else important, you seem to take that opportunity to stir up trouble. This is *one* time you'd better walk straight. I mean it, John. Make up your mind right now not to do the least little thing that could ruin Susie's wedding."

He looked me straight in the eye.

"Mom, you don't have to worry. I'll do what I'm supposed to. I want the wedding to be nice too."

I was convinced.

"Now will you fix me some lunch?"

Susie's graduation rolled around. Wearing her brand-new Phi Beta Kappa key, she walked proudly across the stage with the other honor graduates. Bob and I swelled with pride, but a sardonic remark from John brought us back to earth.

"You might as well enjoy all these honors, because it's probably not gonna happen again in this family."

Bob protested. "That's not necessarily so. You and Mike can do just as well as Susie, or better."

"I don't know about Mike, but I don't have any intention of trying," said this bewildering boy. "I told you I'd set my goal—a respectable C average."

John's year-end grades proved that he was living up to his self-established standard. For some youngsters, a C average would be thrilling, but for John, with his ability, it was a sellout.

As soon as we returned home, the wedding excitement set in in full force. Presents began to arrive. The phone rang constantly. Every day there were myriad things to see to. I put Mike and John to work moving furniture and building shelves to display the gifts. Bob kept them busy cutting grass, trimming bushes, cleaning the terrace, washing porch furniture. They had little time to get into mischief.

After a particularly strenuous day, a week before the wedding, Bob and I went to bed early. At midnight the door of our room opened softly. I opened my eyes to see Susie silhouetted against the light from the hall.

"What is it, honey?"

She tiptoed in to whisper, "Mama, are you asleep?"

"Well, not now."

"Can you come in my room for a minute?"

"Is it really important? Can't it wait till morning?"

"I don't think so. You'd better come."

Aching with tiredness, I got up, put on my robe, and followed her.

"What's the matter?"

"I think you'd better go downstairs to see about John. After I went to bed I heard a noise in the den, so I went down to see what it was. John was sitting there in the dark, smoking a joint and getting high. He's all worked up—just like that night when he came back from prep school and we sat up all night talking. He wants to talk to you."

"For crying out loud! He'll just have to wait. I'm worn out."

"Mama, I really think you should go. He's all nervous and upset. He says he won't go to bed until he can talk to you."

The last thing I wanted was a chat with my son the pothead. But mother love—or my need for martyrdom—won out. True to form, I went downstairs to deal with the trouble and let Bob sleep. When there was a problem, the kids invariably bypassed Dad and came to Mom. Feeling thoroughly resentful, I realized suddenly that I'd taught them to do it!

And once again, Susan had been chosen as the go-between. The boys found it less scary to share things with Susan than to tell us directly. They counted on her to deliver the bad news, and she always saw that they got the help they needed.

When I walked into the smoke-filled den, John was sprawled out defiantly on the sofa. He had on a pair of ragged jeans and a tie-dyed T-shirt, with a dirty red bandanna tied around his head. His eyes were puffy and red. The television flickered dimly in the corner, the sound turned too low to be heard. A burned-out roach lay in the ashtray; he was finishing a second one.

"You're high, aren't you, son?"

"You might say I've got a buzz going."

I was surprised at my own calmness. "I don't believe I want to talk to you tonight. I'll be glad to talk to you tomorrow when you're straight. Go on to bed, John."

I was making progress. I was not haranguing or arguing. I did not accuse or denigrate. I accepted the reality I saw, and even made a brief attempt to back out of the role I had always played in our interactions.

"I'm not going to bed, Mom," he declared intensely, folding his arms. "You're gonna talk to me! I've got a lot of things to say to you, and I plan to say them *now*."

"All right, John," I sighed. "I'll listen for an hour, and then I'm going to bed. I need a lot of rest these days."

"Okay." John was belligerent, but seemed close to tears.

"What is it you want to talk about, son?"

"It's about you and Dad, and me and my life."

"Well, go on."

"You won't let me be myself. You're always trying to put your number off on me, wanting me to be just like Dad, making me go to college and trying to get me to go to medical school, making me go to church when I hate it, making me get haircuts when I hate that, staying on my case all the time about cleaning up my room, about my friends, about the way I spend my time. You won't even let me have a car!" John's old car had long ago given up the ghost.

He paused for a long trembling drag on his joint; then his manner changed from accusing to scornful.

"You came down to school and put on that ridiculous scene with Dean Smith. I guess you don't know he's been laughing at you ever since. He thought it was a scream, you getting all worked up about me smoking a little dope! What a laugh! You don't have any idea how ridiculous you looked down there!"

Finding no hook to hang on to in this free-form outpouring, I just listened.

"Another thing is living here. You're always putting off jobs on me that you don't want to do—vacuuming, mowing the grass, weeding, raking leaves. It's like I'm a slave! I don't feel this is my home. I feel like a slave and you're the rulers! I get all the dirty work and none of the rewards!"

"I'm sorry you feel that way. You can move out any time you like."

"No, I can't, either, dammit. If I move out, you and Dad won't send me back to school." A self-righteous note crept into his voice. "I want a good education."

"You can get an education on your own, son. Plenty of kids work their way through school."

"You know I can't make enough money to do it. Anyway, I think your and Dad's attitude stinks." John was adept at getting off the hot seat; in seconds, he had adroitly turned the spotlight away from himself and onto us, putting me on the defensive. "You act like you're perfect. You both think you're so holy and righteous! You get that look on your face that says, 'You're nothing but a piece of dirt.' And Dad goes into his I'm-the-captain-of-this-ship-and-you'll-do-as-I-say number. Most of the time I feel like hauling off and punching you both. You don't have any idea how much self-control it takes to keep me from doing it."

Did John know his behavior frequently produced the same reaction in me?

He went on and on in the same vein. There was little productive that I could say. John's deeper feelings were apparently stirred; he seemed to want someone just to be there with him. I listened until he'd unloaded most of his emotional poisons and calmed down a bit. The only thing I got out of our talk was the realization that deep inside, John still had feelings, he was not invulnerable, he did care about what was happening to him and to our family. He came across as a frightened little boy, in spite of his bravado. He was riding the tiger and had forgotten how to dismount.

The buzz wore off, and John finally gave up and went to bed. So did I, but I lay awake until dawn, renewing my determination to find some kind of help that would bring him back from his self-erected prison. When the alarm clock woke Bob, I told him about the encounter. He left for the office with the old beaten look on his face. I turned over for a few hours' fitful rest. Finally at noon, I got up, showered, and dressed. John was still asleep.

A new plan was taking shape in my mind. I opened the phone book to the Yellow Pages under *Drug Abuse & Addiction—Information & Treatment*. There was only one listing: Substance Abuse Center—Family and

Individual Counseling. I dialed the number, noting familiar waves of anxiety in my innards.

"SAC—Substance Abuse Center," a pleasant voice answered.

"Hello. I'm calling to ask about your counseling services. I have an eighteen-year-old son who's having a problem with drugs. Could he get some counseling help at your center?"

"Yes indeed. We have several excellent counselors on our staff. Any one of them will be glad to work with him."

"We may have trouble getting him to cooperate. He's already been in counseling once, and that counselor told him she couldn't help him unless he wanted to stop doing drugs. I don't think he wants to stop yet, but my husband and I aren't willing to leave it there. We want to do everything we can to try to help him."

"I understand. The best beginning would be for you and your husband to bring your son in for an interview."

"Fine. Say in about two weeks? My daughter's wedding is next week. We'd like to have that out of the way before we start."

"Our first opening is about that far ahead anyway. I'll set it up for two weeks from today. At 3:00 in the afternoon?"

"Wonderful. We'll be there. White is the name—Dr. and Mrs. White. Our son's name is John."

"We'll see you then, Mrs. White. And in the meantime, enjoy your daughter's wedding. Don't give up hope. I'm sure things will work out."

Susie had overhead the conversation.

"Great move, Mama! You *have* to do something. Maybe this will be what John needs, since Dr. Lannon bombed out."

Mike had been listening too. He wasn't optimistic. "It won't do any good. Knowing John, he'll figure out a way to get out of going, just like he did the last time."

His pessimism didn't faze me. Someday we'd hit on the right combination—that hope kept me going.

When Bob came home, he was encouraged that I'd taken this step. We agreed to say nothing to John yet. It was important to keep him on an even keel until after the wedding, but this effort added a new note of tension to the proceedings.

When the prewedding parties began, everything seemed to be under control. Susie's dress and veil arrived, as did the bridesmaids' dresses. Bob and the boys had their final fittings. Lisa, Susie's roommate and maid of honor, flew in to stay with us. Dave and his family drove in and took rooms at the hotel.

Susie and Dave were joyful, confident that they were embarking on a lasting and fulfilling marriage. Bob and I had not celebrated anything for so long, it was wonderful to share this happy time with family and friends.

Dave and Susie's friends were a lively, amusing bunch, and they included Mike and John in all their doings. At the parties, there were always drinks; the boys' glasses were filled, along with the others. At the rehearsal dinner they made graceful toasts, laughed appropriately at the jokes, and flirted with the girls. John was peppier than we'd seen him in ages.

On the day of the wedding, things went swimmingly. The weather was perfect; the church was lovely; the wedding party looked splendid. Dave, John, and Mike were a tall, handsome trio; Susan was a picture of radiant happiness in her long white dress and veil. The ceremony was appropriately solemn and beautiful. Afterward, the cake was cut and the bride and groom fed each other the traditional gooey pieces. Susan threw her bouquet and Lisa caught it.

But when Dave made ready to toss Susie's garter, there was a hitch: Brother John was nowhere to be found. The newlyweds were eager to change clothes and make their getaway, so the search was abandoned; the others grabbed for the garter without him.

John was still missing when the bride and groom dashed excitedly out to their car and drove off in a shower of rice. Susie waved until they were out of sight. Everyone lingered for a few minutes, looking after the car and smiling fondly—everyone but Bob and me. We were wondering where the hell John was.

As we reentered the clubhouse, he came sauntering down the hall from the men's room. The look on his face was by now thoroughly familiar—the expressionless mask of the pothead. For once, Bob recognized it too. John had been in the bathroom getting high.

"Susie and Dave are gone," Bob told him brusquely. "Susie wanted to tell you good-bye, and you weren't there when Dave threw the garter."

"Sorry," said John with a shrug.

"Sorry is right," said Bob angrily. "Sorry is all you ever are! John, sorry isn't enough any more."

"Bob, shhh! Not now, honey." I tried to distract him. "People are still waiting to speak to us."

Bob said the appropriate things to our guests, but when we were home at last, he was ready to explode.

"John!" he shouted upstairs as John disappeared into his room. "I want you down here!"

"Now?"

"*Now!*"

"Can't I take off this monkey suit first?"

"Get down here right now! My patience is hanging by a thread!"

John came down. We three sat down for what must have been the hundredth such talk.

"John, I'm laying down the law!" said Bob tersely. "Your mother and I can't accept things as they stand any longer. You defeated our efforts to get help for you at Chambers, but you're not going to keep on blocking us."

"Dr. Lannon said there wasn't any use—"

"Shut up! I don't want to hear anything you or Dr. Lannon has to say. For once you're doing the listening. Have you got that straight?"

"Yes sir."

"All right. A week from today, you're going with your mother and me to the Substance Abuse Center downtown. You'll be seen there regularly for counseling for the rest of this summer. That's the only condition under which you'll be allowed to live at home any longer, or go back to Chambers this fall. Is that clear?"

"Yes sir." It was impossible to read the thoughts behind that stone face.

I was longing to say something that would let John know how much we loved him and how hard it was to continue living with him this way, but no words came. I sat in silence, close to tears. He looked at me with what I interpreted as disdain, then stared back at Bob, saying nothing.

Bob dismissed him. "All right, son, that's all. Go take off the suit. Hang it up, and stay out of my sight for a while."

In truth, poor John really had done the best he could. He'd done his part before and during the wedding. He'd been pleasant and obliging, and Susie's wedding had gone off without a hitch; the day was a thoroughly happy one for her and for Dave. John had gone without his chemicals for as long as possible at that stage of the game. Now it was up to Bob and me to forge ahead with our new plan.

Our interview at SAC was easier than the earlier one with Dean Smith. Glenn, the director, was a good listener. Bob began our story as John sat in annoyed silence. He drummed his fingers, crossed and uncrossed his legs, jiggled a foot, stared into the distance, sighed loudly.

Bob's emotional tension finally broke, and he blurted out, "Glenn, I just love this boy so much, I care so damn much about him, it's killing me to watch him destroy himself!"

To my astonishment, sympathetic tears brimmed up in John's eyes and swift color rose to his cheeks. Glenn spotted the break in composure too. Hope rose once more. Here again was proof that John still had some normal human feelings, however deeply buried.

At the end of the interview, Glenn outlined his recommendations.

"John, I'd like you to meet regularly for counseling with Dr. Luther, our chief psychologist. He's had years of experience with troubled youngsters. I'm sure he'll be able to help. Are you willing to cooperate?"

"I guess so," John said indifferently.

"Doctor and Mrs. White, I'd like you to come in on a regular basis for conferences with Elaine, another counselor on our staff. The two counselors will confer frequently and relay progress reports. Is that agreeable?"

"We'll do whatever you say," said Bob.

Glenn added, "There's one more thing—I'd like John to come in for some psychological testing. We always like to rule out any serious psychological problems before we begin counseling."

*How serious does it have to be?* asked one of the two little voices inside my head. In four years' time, we'd seen John through three automobile accidents, two arrests and court appearances, a year of probation, untold family conflicts, repeated episodes of drunkenness and drug intoxication, and a steady decline in academic performance.

But then the other little voice took up the debate: *These are the experts. You know nothing. You've placed yourself in their hands. You must follow their advice.*

Before we left Glenn's office, John came up with at least one obstacle to our plan, as Mike had predicted. "Can I say something here?"

"Sure, John," said Glenn.

"Nobody's mentioned the fact that I have a job on a farm this summer. I start work Monday. How do you suggest I keep these appointments if I have to work every day?"

"Your health is far more important than a job or anything else," Bob declared. "Glenn can give you a letter stating that you must be seen here regularly. If your boss won't let you keep your appointments, you'll have to look for another job. It's that simple."

John gave up the argument, hearing the resolution in Bob's voice.

And so we started another long hot summer. Mike and John were working on the farm together. Mike was charged with letting us know how John was behaving; he reported nothing out of the way. To our surprise, John showed up without fail for his appointments at SAC. He told us he liked Dr. Luther and their sessions were going well.

In the evenings John went out with Paul, a new friend.

Paul was in his middle twenties. He had no job, nor did he go to school. He just lived at home with his parents and "hung out." Paul looked like a waste case to me—his eyes were always red-rimmed, he usually had a couple days' growth of skimpy beard, and he had the same utterly bland facade as Angelo and the other older boys John had gravitated toward over the years.

He went out with Paul almost every night—"to listen to tapes." He assured us he was staying off dope. But after he'd been in counseling for more than a month, John came in one night unquestionably stoned. Next morning I confronted him—confrontations were still my department. He admitted being high, but he was repentant.

"I know you feel bad that I've had a slip, Mom. I feel bad about it too. I plan to talk about it with Dr. Luther this afternoon. Don't worry. He can help me."

Really, the only slip John had made was in letting me find out. All that summer, he conned us like a pro. He never stopped using pot, often smoking during breaks on the farm. A fellow worker who grew enough for his own use shared it with John and occasionally with Mike, so Mike didn't give the game away. John was invariably high when he kept his appointments with Luther, and since Luther had never seen him any other way, he was as thoroughly deceived as the rest of us.

Clever John just went through the motions. He knew how far he could go without being kicked out of the house, and the exact degree of compliance necessary to keep us feeding him and paying his bills. He even talked his way out of a fender-bender with our car when he was stoned. The situation didn't "feel" right to Bob and me, but our self-confidence had been so thoroughly undermined, we didn't trust our feelings. Nor was there enough hard evidence to convince us not to send John back to college. We were afraid his alternative would be to move in with Paul—and that was too discouraging even to think about.

At our SAC meetings with Elaine, she assured us that John was making progress. I couldn't see much change. I finally got worked up enough to stop in to see Dr. Luther during one of John's appointments. The receptionist didn't want to interrupt their counseling session, but I insisted. I made my way upstairs to Dr. Luther's office, knocked on the door, and just walked in. John and Dr. Luther seemed quite surprised to see me. Before my courage failed, I spoke out.

"Doctor Luther, I'd like a few minutes of your time. John's dad and I don't see a whole lot of change in John. I'd appreciate hearing your evaluation of his progress at this point." John had then been in counseling for about six weeks.

"John, would you mind waiting downstairs for a little while?" the counselor requested smoothly. John left without comment, and I took a seat across the desk from the burly bearded man.

"Mrs. White, I don't believe you have a thing to worry about," began Dr. Luther as he toyed with a pen. "John's coming along all right. Judging from his psychological tests, I'd have to say he is probably the brightest person I've ever worked with. We did detect a slight tendency to self-destructive behavior, but we don't believe it's a serious cause for alarm."

I still wasn't satisfied. "But how do you feel he's progressing in terms of his drug problem? We've seen very little change in his attitude at home, and I'm sure you know about his slip."

"You must know that nearly all kids nowadays smoke a little grass and drink some beer. John is no different from his peers, Mrs. White. He's just trying out his independence, feeling his oats."

Those thoughts of self-doubt began to run through my mind again: *Am I crazy? Am I making a big deal out of nothing? Is John perfectly normal? What's wrong with me? Why can't I trust these people?*

Doctor Luther went on. "Many nights when I go home, I lie awake, worrying about some of these youngsters I work with, wondering what in God's name will become of them, whether they'll even survive. I've never lost a moment's sleep on John's account. John's going to be fine."

I thanked him for his time and left, more discouraged than ever. If John was fine, something must be dreadfully wrong with me. Was there any solution to this maddening puzzle?

John came home for supper wearing a triumphant grin. "Thanks for coming down to SAC, Mom. You really helped me out. Now Dr. Luther understands what I have to go through, trying to live at home and satisfy you."

And so once again we were stuck—committed to a form of help that wasn't helping, wondering why we couldn't make any progress; afraid to give up the counseling and afraid to turn John loose on his own; hating the tyranny that his behavior exercised over our household but powerless to release its hold on us.

But although we made no breakthrough during that unhappy summer, some very important seeds would soon be sown.

I saw a morning television show that featured adolescent graduates of a residential chemical-dependency treatment program. These young people and their parents were tremendously impressive. They talked frankly of the misery alcohol/drug dependency had caused in their lives and spoke eagerly about the wonderful prospects opening up to them in their recovery.

A toll-free phone number was shown at the program's end, and I called to request information. We still spoke of John's difficulties as "a problem with drugs." I still thought of an addict as someone with needle tracks on the arms, a flophouse failure who'd hold up a grocery store for $20. John certainly didn't fit that picture. But the fact that I made the call at all represented an admission of sorts that he might be addicted.

The person who took my call asked probing questions: Are there behavior problems? Does he have trouble getting along with other family members? Is he irritable and moody, prone to fits of anger and violence? Has he been in trouble with the law? To all these, I had to say yes.

The questions went on: Is he having trouble in school? Has he dropped out of school? Have you noticed money or valuables disappearing? Has he run away from home? These questions confused me. John had long been a school behavior problem, but his grades remained acceptable. He had never taken money or anything valuable, though he occasionally "lost" things. He had threatened to run away, but never did. So to all these questions, I thought I could answer no.

Denial took over again, and I began to minimize the problem. I told the counselor I was just asking for information, our problem wasn't a serious one, and we really didn't need anything as drastic as inpatient treatment.

"All right, ma'am. But if things get worse, and they probably will, you know how to reach us."

"Yes, thanks, but I'm sure they won't."

Long afterward, the faces of the kids on that show came back to me again and again—eager, lively, healthy and glowing. I couldn't imagine that they'd ever been like my sullen, hostile, apathetic son.

A packet of literature arrived in the mail a few days later as a result of my call. I read it, then stuck it away in a drawer. No, John wasn't dependent on drugs. He just wouldn't stop messing with them. It was bound to be an emotional problem.

In a bookstore I spotted a book, *Toma Tells It Straight—With Love,* written by a former undercover policeman who now lectures kids about drugs. I bought it.

Toma did tell it straight, straighter than I wanted to hear it. He itemized signs of drug dependency: behavioral changes, self-imposed isolation from the family, new friends who are slick and secretive, hostility, rebelliousness, disrespect, phone callers who won't identify themselves, immaturity, lack of motivation, dropping grades, loss of interest in hobbies and extracurricular activities, auto accidents, red and light-sensitive eyes, habitual use of eyedrops, mood swings, depression and loneliness, manic excitement, rages, dreadful language, habitual lying, suicide threats—and in John we had seen it all!

Toma's advice was tough: "Confront your kid as soon as possible. Every day you wait is going to cost him." Well, we had done this, at least in a way. "You must separate them from their drugs," he said. Here we fell down. John was walking the streets every day and had the use of our car to drive to work.

Toma recommended isolating abusers immediately from any outside contact for at least thirty days, to clear the drugs out of their systems and allow a return of rational thinking. And we had done that. Where we failed was in not following through afterward.

"If a kid hasn't left [home] voluntarily when he's out of school or of age," Toma wrote, "it's probably because he's afraid to. He may realize that he hasn't anything going for him." This could explain why John hadn't completely blocked our efforts to get him into counseling, why he hadn't left home altogether. "He may try to talk you into paying for his college. . . . Don't do it. . . . Don't do anything to help him continue living with drugs." Such good advice!

And yet I hadn't the courage to follow it. I told Bob what I had read, but neither of us was ready to take such drastic measures. In spite of all the evidence, we were still resisting the idea that our boy was an addict.

At summer's end we had our summary conference at SAC. Elaine reassured us that John's counseling was successful. He was basically a healthy person, and there was no reason he shouldn't return to college.

"Just try treating him more like an adult," she told us as we got up to leave. "I think you'll be surprised how well he responds."

Luther's advice to John was equally misguided and, for an addict, totally absurd: "Just keep your drugs under control, son. It's only when you drink too much or smoke too much grass that things get out of hand. If you watch yourself, you'll be fine. Good luck!"

John was happy to shake the muscular hand Luther extended. To him it represented an expert's permission to keep on raising hell.

We drove John back to Chambers at the opening of school. He was uncharacteristically energetic as he hauled his stereo equipment into the dorm. Bob and I followed with awkward loads of coathangers.

"White! What's happening, man?" A long-haired, not especially clean young man in the hallway slapped John on the back.

"Not much, man. Oh, Adam, these are my folks. Mom and Dad, this is Adam."

"Hi, Adam," I said.

"Hello, Adam," said Bob.

"Yeah. Hi." Adam gave an offhand wave.

"What'd you do this summer, man?" asked John.

"It was wild, man. We went on tour with the Grateful Dead—out to California, up to Red Rocks, New York, everywhere. Man, it was really something. What'd you do?"

"Busted my butt all summer working on a farm. Say, is Lance back yet?"

"Lance? Lance Johnson? No way! He flunked out!"

"Are you serious? Lance flunked out?"

"Yeah, he busted out. I thought you knew it. Weren't you guys rooming together?"

"Yeah, we were gonna room together this year too. I didn't hear a thing from him except a card from somewhere up North. He was following the Dead too."

"Yeah, I know. I saw him in D.C. That's how I knew he busted out of school. He told me he was going to State U."

"Bummer, man!" John said lightheartedly. He was much less disturbed by this piece of news than I would have been.

"What will you do for a roommate, son?" I asked.

"No problem! I'll just look around for somebody else. No sweat. It'll work out."

Sure enough, in less than fifteen minutes John had found somebody to live with him—a clean-cut, husky wrestler named Will. This young man had a ready smile and a good firm handshake. The mere sight of him raised our hopes of a wholesome school year for John. We told our son good-bye with relief and left for home.

Mike was even happier to have John gone this year than he had been the year before. He was now old enough to drive, so he could use the car occasionally. In John's absence, Mike usually lived up to our expectations, behaviorwise. He was doing well in high school and went around now with a crowd of great kids. They were fresh-faced, enthusiastic, always in and out of the house, friendly and open, a marked contrast to John's skulking associates.

It had been a hectic, exhausting summer—Susan's graduation, then the wedding, and afterward our absorption with John and his problem. We appreciated a return to domestic peace and quiet. Weekends were bearable again. On Friday nights we knew Mike was at the local high school football game, that he would come in on time and not smell of beer or dope. On Saturday night he usually had a date or went to a party; his current crowd had their parties at home with parental supervision. And our car remained intact.

The news from Susie and Dave was glowing. Susie had found a good job and Dave had received a promotion. They loved their cozy apartment in a nice old neighborhood and were making lots of new friends. Having two of our youngsters doing well was a fine feeling.

But with Susie out of school, we had no source of information about John's behavior. We could rarely get him by phone; when we called, Will said John was visiting in someone else's room. But when we called the numbers he gave us, he wasn't there either. And he never phoned us unless he wanted money or something else we could supply.

We kept his allowance at a bare minimum—just enough for haircuts, toilet articles, an occasional date, and a pizza once in a while. We were certainly not giving him enough for those things, plus drugs and drinks. But John found a way around his dilemma. He simply left off the haircuts, toilet articles, dates, and pizzas and spent every cent on drinks or drugs. When he ran out of money, one of his buddies usually was willing to share his stash. Campus parties were plentiful, and free beer could always be found somewhere. So our attempt to control the use of chemicals by withholding funds was defeated.

When a buddy dropped John off at home for Thanksgiving, we were stunned at the change in his appearance. He had gained at least twenty pounds and was bulging out of his clothes. His hair was long, ragged, and unclean. He sported dark glasses and a wide-brimmed straw hat, bent down in front with a raccoon tail hanging in back. His wallet was on a chain, and his feet were crammed into cowboy boots. He came in the house carrying a full six-pack of beer and the remaining two cans of another. He'd drunk four beers on the seventy-mile drive.

"Hi, Mom, Dad." The fumes on his breath were noticeable. "Sure is good to be home. Dad, can I borrow the car for a few minutes?"

"You just walked in the door. Why do you need the car right away?"

"Well, tomorrow's Thanksgiving, you know. The stores will be closed. I want to get some beer for the weekend."

Another tip-off, if we'd realized it—the addict worries about running out. John had laid his plans with forethought. He knew he could use beer at our house without causing a ruckus, and he was making certain his supply was secure. Bob let him have the keys.

A kaleidoscopic blur of questions whirled through my mind: *Is John sick? Why else would he look like this? Why would he go out of his way to look and act like a bum? Why is he drinking so much?*

But when he returned with two more six-packs, the one question that came out of my mouth sounded inane even to me.

"Are you having a party, John?"

He laughed scornfully. "A party? What kind of a party could I have with just two six-packs? Come off it, Mom. This is my vacation! I deserve a little relaxation."

"If you drink all that beer, you'll definitely be relaxed."

It was no wonder he looked at me with contempt. "I imagine you and Dad will have a few drinks. You usually do on holidays. I saw a couple of bottles of wine in the kitchen just now when I was putting the beer in the fridge. And then you always have your scotch and soda."

*Turn the spotlight on somebody else; get if off yourself.* Years of practice had made John very good at that.

# CHAPTER SEVEN

# A Girl and a Getaway

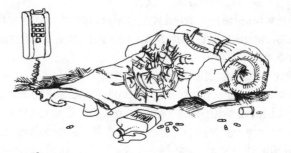

_____*A* complete blank—that's what much of John's second school year was for us. We saw him occasionally during vacations; otherwise his life was a mystery. We knew nothing of his friends or activities or courses, except for the usual mediocre grades that came in the mail. We finally gave up trying to reach him by phone. He never wrote, and our letters went unopened or unread.

Those same weeks and months were also a hazy blur to John, as he groped his way in a chronically altered state of mind. He got high on pot several times a day, and he got drunk many nights and every weekend. He often vomited, but he kept on drinking. He ate eccentrically—skipped meals at times for a day or more, went on eating binges at other times. Mexican and Oriental food were his favorites—the spicier the better.

We knew none of this. John couldn't allow any interference, for chemicals had become his obsession, his whole reason for being. The only thing that mattered was having enough to fuel his now-permanent high.

But he surprised us during Christmas vacation. When

he wasn't sleeping or out with his friends, John spent hours wrapping wadded-up T-shirts with twine and stirring great bubbling kettles of dye on the kitchen stove. Tie-dyeing became his mania. He did it in the same way he did everything else—full throttle.

John is a compulsive personality. He takes up each new craze with a passion and pursues it fanatically, setting everything else aside until the obsession burns itself out and he falls under the spell of the next one.

As he gained experience, his designs became singular and intricate. I knew that tie-dyed T-shirts were a Deadhead trademark; John said these were Christmas gifts for his friends.

In the midst of this dyeing, Mike sauntered into the kitchen.

"What's all this ugly mess?" He indicated the dripping shirts that hung over the sink.

"They're tie-dyed T-shirts, asshole," responded John.

Mike's jaw tightened; he shouldered John roughly out of the way.

"Watch who you're shoving, big boy."

"*You* watch it! If Mom wasn't standing here, I'd kick your butt." Mike was now taller than John by several inches and his equal in weight. John talked a big game, but he really didn't want to tangle with Mike.

"Boys, I don't like your language, and I'll thank you to act your age."

"John's acting his age—three." Mike bent over to look in the refrigerator.

John shoved Mike so hard that his nose banged painfully against the edge of a shelf.

"Goddammit, John, I've had all I'm gonna take from you." Mike grabbed John's shirt; it ripped. John picked up a heavy skillet. The pot of boiling dye was in danger.

"Boys! Knock it off right this minute!" I screeched, shoving them apart.

But John couldn't leave well enough alone. "Mikey has to have Mom take up for him."

"John, get out of this kitchen," I ordered.

"I'll be glad to get out, as long as this asshole stays in it." He gave Mike the high sign on his way out the door.

Mike slammed the refrigerator door.

"You see what a jerk he is. I hate his guts. Mom, why do you let him get away with that stuff? If I were you, I'd have him put in a mental hospital. That's where he belongs."

"Just drop it, Mike. He'll be back at school soon."

"The sooner the better." Mike carried a handful of raw hot dogs out to the back porch, where he wolfed them down in a resentful silence.

I felt degraded, helpless, totally out of control. Trying to keep so many volatile temperaments from exploding was an impossible job. Like Mike, I could hardly wait for John to go back to school.

After things were quiet, I noticed that one of the dripping shirts was a very small one, dyed in pretty pastel shades of lavender, pink, and turquoise.

A considerably calmer John came back into the kitchen after a bit. The pupils of his eyes appeared very large and black, but I didn't risk a comment about that.

"Who's this little shirt for?"

"A girl I know."

"What's her name?"

"Amy."

The first-name-only habit of the young irritates me. We regularly fielded calls from people who refused to leave a first name, much less a last one. "I'll call back later," they always said. In the drug culture, it is necessary to keep your identity and your message private.

"Amy who?"

"You wouldn't know her."

It was John's first mention of a girl since early high school days. My curiosity was aroused, but he meant to keep his secrets to himself.

Actually, the tie-dyeing gave me cause for hope. At least he was doing something creative, instead of just sleeping, eating, smoking, drinking, and grousing at the rest of the family. After he went back to school, taking the shirts with him, I enjoyed remembering the watery swirls of color, his excitement as he unwrapped the twine, his pleasure at creating something unique.

Little by little we heard more about Amy, and finally John asked to bring her home for a weekend. We were curious, to say the least. They arrived in Amy's nearly new, well-kept car. She was at the wheel, a petite brunette, attractively dressed in Earth Mother chic. Her manner was friendly and warm. Obviously fond of John, she clung to his arm and nestled close whenever possible.

John was proud of his new relationship, eager for our approval. When Amy went upstairs to unpack he pressed us for our opinion.

"Mom, how do you like Amy?"

"She seems really nice, as far as I can tell."

"Dad, don't you think Amy's beautiful?"

"She's very nice-looking, son."

John craved more superlatives, sweeping approval. Our acceptance of Amy was tied in with his own self-esteem. We said as many complimentary things as we honestly could on such short acquaintance, but he wanted more and said as much.

"*I* think she's *gorgeous*! I don't know what's wrong with

you if you can't see it. And she's just as nice as she is beautiful, too."

"Okay, John," Bob said. "It's obvious you really like her. After we get to know Amy, maybe we can learn to care for her as much as you do."

Amy's visit was pleasant enough. She fit in with our family routine, offered to set the table, chatted in a relaxed way, helped with the dishes, and sat down with a book when nothing else was going on. But she really came to life in John's presence. The chemistry between them was obvious. They held hands, gazed into each other's eyes, whispered and giggled, talked baby talk. It was a new experience to see John in the throes of infatuation.

Amy seemed to like John's dominating ways. Whatever he wanted to do was fine with her. She hardly ever expressed a preference, but went along happily with his whims. She had a stock response: "Whatever you want to do, John."

When the weekend was over, Bob voiced the very question I was about to ask him.

"Didn't you think Amy was terribly passive? She seemed like putty in John's hands."

"I thought so too, but maybe we're being too judgmental. Maybe she just wants to please him."

"Pleasing people is okay," said Bob, "so long as you know your own mind. This girl reminded me of a marionette, with John working the strings."

Amy frequently came home with John after that. We were happy to share in his life again, even on a superficial level. We enjoyed having the two of them around and tried to forget the tormenting scenes of the past. Amy had a civilizing influence on John; he kept himself cleaner, paid more attention to his clothes, was more interested in doing things with the family.

Their activities fell into a pattern. John called the shots, and as long as Amy bought into his plans, things went smoothly. But whenever she held out for her own desires, or tried to keep him from doing something he wanted to do, John blew up. Their relationship worked only as long as John played the tyrant and Amy the submissive slave.

"John, it worries me that you show so little consideration for Amy," I told him. "Sometimes you're just plain rude, and you don't give a hoot about her feelings. You certainly weren't brought up to treat women like that."

"You only see one side of it. You don't have any idea how much she bugs me. When she's here, she acts like little Miss Goody-good, but at school she's always whining and nagging."

"Nagging you about what?"

"For one thing, every time I go over to Gary's, she calls up and starts bugging me to spend time with her instead. Gary gives me a lot of grief about it: 'Little John's mother is calling him home!' It really pisses me off, and I tell her so. That's just one example."

The essential element John left out of his story was that Gary was his chief party partner. Amy hated the way John acted when he was using drugs or drinking. Her calls to Gary's room were attempts to control the partying, but they produced the opposite result. John resisted Amy's efforts as vehemently as he had resisted ours. When Amy begged him not to drink or get high, John proved his independence by drinking more and getting high twice as often.

He *had* to drink and do drugs for another compelling reason—to quiet his own nagging inner voices: *She's right, John. You shouldn't do it. You know it's wrong. But you can't stop, can you, John? It would kill you to stop.*

*You know it, and we know it. You've got to keep on, or else
you'll die.*

He actually was a slave to chemicals, and he couldn't
stand this knowledge. When he was drunk or stoned, the
voices fell silent for a while.

Months later, we discovered why Amy had been drawn
to John in the first place. A member of her immediate
family was an alcoholic, and the expression she saw in
John's eyes was the very one her beloved relative so often
wore. John seemed comfortable and familiar. It was like
coming home.

This is a totally predictable response among children of
addicted parents. They are drawn to addicted lovers like
filings to a magnet, yet they don't understand why. They
try subconsciously to duplicate their early model of
"normal" family life, knowing no other kind. Amy was
drawn like a delicate little moth to the only flame she
recognized as love—the craziness and emotional turmoil
of alcohol addiction.

Her behavior during that period was typical of someone
who loves an addict. She felt guilty. She blamed herself
for John's excesses, just as we had blamed ourselves, but
she couldn't admit that guilt to anyone. And since she
assumed that John's condition was her fault, therefore it
must be her responsibility to straighten him out. We were
clinging to the same delusion—that it was only a matter of
finding the right combination of controls.

She nagged, scolded, begged, pleaded, promised, gave
in, clammed up, isolated herself, went running back, had
hysterics, cried, yelled, drank and got high too—all in the
hope of halting John's self-destructive progress. None of
it worked, because neither John nor Amy had any control
over his disease.

John's life was centered totally on chemicals. Amy was

only a peripheral part of that life. If he had been forced to choose between chemicals and Amy, he would have chosen chemicals, and Amy knew it. Her affection was valuable to John just as long as she didn't interfere.

So she sat by miserably as John got high, hoping her watchfulness would somehow protect him. She suffered his abuses, telling herself she deserved them. She went to Grateful Dead concerts and pretended to be happy while everybody got stoned. She drank with John, smoked dope with him, tripped on 'shrooms and acid, trying all the while to find a way to touch his soul.

John was unreachable. Drugs were his defense against the world, a defense he could not surrender. Amy tried with all her might to storm the fortress, but in the end she was as unsuccessful as everybody else. John's addiction was stronger than any power that besieged it.

Finally Amy took a gutsy step. Miserable with John and miserable without him, she somehow found the courage to leave Chambers and go abroad to study. It was a colossal leap for freedom.

John responded indifferently. "Okay with me, if that's what she wants to do."

After she left, he came home for the summer and got a job tending bar at a country club—the fox in charge of the henhouse! We let him live at home, after exacting a promise of no more emotional firestorms. John assured us that everything would be cool.

In spite of his addiction, John had learned a great deal about getting along with others when it suited his purposes to do so. That summer at home, he was agreeable, cheerful, and polite.

He had a disturbing habit, however. He would come home from work, mix himself a huge Bloody Mary and down it in five or ten minutes, then follow it immediately with a second—all this *before* an evening out. More than once we found a couple of dozen empty beer cans in our garbage bin. We knew John was drinking a lot, but we were used to alcohol.

"All college kids drink beer," we rationalized.

John did his drugs away from home that summer. We never saw any concrete evidence, nor could we ever tell that he was drunk or stoned. He made it to work on time every day, did his job to the satisfaction of his boss, kept himself clean and tidy, even sported a neat haircut. From our point of view, things looked good. We conveniently managed to overlook his compulsive drinking.

At the dinner table one evening, a new topic came up.

"Dad, I'd like to talk to you about something," John said in his most earnest manner. "I need a car."

"You had one, son, and you tore it up."

"I know I did. But I'm a lot older now, and a lot more responsible. I could really use a car at school, and I'd like to have it by the end of the summer, to go camping with my friends over Labor Day, before school starts."

"John, your driving record is no good. I've been paying exorbitant insurance premiums for the last three years."

"I know, Dad, it hasn't been good in the past. But I haven't had a wreck in almost three years. This really means a lot to me. I've got to prove myself some time."

John had just turned nineteen. It was true that he hadn't had a wreck in more than two years. His driving was still less than reassuring, but nowhere near as erratic as it once had been.

"Let me think it over. I'll talk to the insurance people to see what it will cost me. I'll let you know what I decide."

"Okay, Dad. But think about it seriously, will you? Give me a chance to prove I'm responsible and mature."

Bob did think about it seriously. Things were apparently going better with John; perhaps he really had earned a new chance. Bob decided a few days later to do the generous thing.

"Here's my offer, John. If you can come up with half the money, I'll make up the other half. You should be able to get a pretty good car by the end of the summer, and maybe you'll take better care of it than you did the last one."

"Gosh, thanks, Dad! I really appreciate your attitude. You can count on me this time for sure. I'll take care of that car just like you take care of yours!"

"We'll see about that. Oh, and one more thing, John—I have to have your word there'll be no drinking and driving. That's a must."

"No problem, Dad. If I want to drink, I'll ride with somebody else. You can count on that, too."

John's energies were galvanized by this new project. He stashed his paychecks in the bank with miserly glee. We supplied food and housing, so he had little to spend money on. His alcohol habit was taken care of, for the most part, by surreptitious drinking on the job, and he had plenty of "friends" who would share drugs when he was low on funds. Bob and I coasted along in blissful ignorance, thinking how well John was coming along.

As his bank account grew, John's plans for the camping trip took shape. He talked about it for weeks and began to pile up gear in his room: sleeping bag, backpack, tent, cooking pots. He and three friends planned to camp in a wilderness area in North Carolina, he said; they would drive from there directly back to Chambers when school opened in the fall.

"We'll need to know exactly where you'll be camping," I told John as he pored over his maps.

"No problem! I'll tell you everything you need to know."

And indeed, one afternoon he handed me a list of names—his friend Gary, a boy named Lew, and a third one called Thad. Not only had he written down first names, but he had supplied last names and phone numbers as well. This was a blue-ribbon day for family communication.

"Thanks, John. I appreciate not having to drag it out of you for once."

"You're welcome," he said magnanimously.

"Now tell me again exactly where you're going."

"I'm picking up Lew and driving to Thad's house in Waynesille. We'll leave the car there, on Spruce Avenue, right up the street from the fire station. From there we plan to backpack up to Mount Pisgah. If you need to find us, you can call Thad's folks. They'll know more or less where we are. But it is a wilderness area—there aren't any telephones!"

"This is Thad's parents' number here, right?"

"Right."

"Okay, I've got all that straight. And then you'll drive back to Chambers the day before school starts?"

"You got it. I'll call you when I get back to school, to let you know I'm okay."

In mid-August John came home from work and tossed his checkbook triumphantly on the kitchen table.

"Check it out—$1,500! That's what I've saved up. Dad says he'll match it. That means I'll have $3,000 to buy my car!"

Bob was amazed when he came home and heard the news. If John had learned to save money, he must be making remarkable progress.

"Are you going to keep your promise about the car?" I asked.

"Sure. A promise is a promise. I'll admit I didn't think he'd come through on his end, but since he's done it, I'll do my part."

Bob and John scanned the classifieds for several days, then drove all over town looking at used cars. They finally settled on a likely choice. It had no air conditioning, but John didn't care. He just wanted that car right now, no questions asked. The day he drove it home, he stayed up long after midnight to install his all-important stereo system, even paying Mike to help. It was the first thing they'd done together in more than two years—another encouraging sign. They bickered a little, but all in all, the job was finished without incident.

The great day of departure finally arrived. John had everything packed the night before, and when daylight came he rolled out of the driveway in great spirits. It was a relief to see him go. John is a high-energy person; you always know he's around, from either the positive or the negative vibrations. I was ready for a little tranquility.

We didn't expect to hear from the campers for a week or more. The week passed quietly, then ten days. The first day of school came and went with no word from John. After two more days, I tried to phone, but no one answered the dorm phone. Several days later, we began to worry in earnest. Finally I telephoned John's dorm again, and this time a student answered.

"May I speak to John White?"

"Who?"

"John White."

"I'm sorry, there's no one by that name on this hall."

"That's funny. Would you mind going down to Room 221 to check? Could you just see whether anybody has moved in?"

I could hear the noisy comings and goings of the boys' dorm as I held the phone, waiting.

"Ma'am? I'm sorry, but that room is empty. No one's living in it." School had then been in session for several days, and registration was long over.

I called the hall where John was supposed to be washing dishes for extra money. It was dinnertime; the phone happened to be answered by John's dorm counselor.

"Is John White there, please?"

"No ma'am, I'm sorry, but John didn't come back to school this year." Although I was on the brink of tears and felt like screaming in terror, I managed to control my voice.

"Are you sure?"

"Yes ma'am, I'm sure. He was supposed to sign in with me to pick up his room key the first of the week, but he hasn't shown up."

It was the worst moment of my life. Crazy thoughts whirled through my head. I mentally summoned up rescue teams and helicopters, dog sleds and mountain climbers. I could see John at the bottom of a crevasse with a broken leg, slowly starving to death, dying of dehydration, wondering whether help would ever come.

I redoubled my efforts, my fingers like spaghetti, my voice breaking unexpectedly. I called John's faculty advisor, the dean of students, anybody and everybody. Nobody knew a thing. It was the bleakest hour I had ever known. *God help us,* I prayed inwardly.

Bob arrived home from the office and quickly became as frightened as I. Neither of us could really think straight, but I did have the names and numbers John had left. Bob stood beside me, struggling against his own anxiety, as I dialed the number for Thad's parents in Waynesville, fingers trembling, heart pounding.

A recorded voice came across the line: "The number you have dialed has been temporarily disconnected." Panic: I must have misdialed. Try again!

"The number you have d—" I hung up, exhausted.

Next I tried Gary's number. It rang and rang, but no one answered. I tried again.

Finally a man said "Hello?" sounding zonked-out and irritable.

"Hello, is this Gary's dad?"

"Yeah. Whaddya want?"

"My name is White." My voice was shaking. "I'm trying to locate my son John. He told me he was going camping a couple of weeks ago with Gary, and we haven't heard from him since. Do you have any idea where they are?"

"Nope. Gary moved out last year to live at the beach. I never see the kid. We don't get along, anyhow. I don't have the vaguest idea where he is or what he's doing."

"Well, thanks all the same," I said, and hung up in despair. The man's tone of voice led me to think that wherever Gary was, he was probably up to no good.

My last hope was the third number on the list, Lew's family. The old urgency was back in my guts in full force. My fingers trembled so much that Bob finally had to dial the number for me. A woman answered.

"Mrs. Grady?" I asked fearfully.

"Yes?"

"My name is Betsy White. You don't know me, but my son John is a friend of Lew's. We haven't heard from John in a couple of weeks, and we're very worried about him. Can you tell me, please, did your boy go camping in the North Carolina mountains with John before Labor Day?"

Her hesitant answer floored me.

"Well, in a way. Lew did go camping with John, but they didn't go to North Carolina. They went to Colorado to a concert by the Grateful Dead."

Relief flooded over me in knee-buckling waves. It had taken me two hours to come up with this information, and I must have aged twenty years.

Mrs. Grady had some questions of her own.

"Mrs. White, perhaps you can help me too. What do you know about these Deadheads? It's all Lew can talk about these days. My husband and I don't like it, but we really don't know much about it." Her voice could have been my own—sad, troubled, bewildered.

"We don't know a lot about it either. We do know there's a lot of drug-taking at the concerts. Some of these youngsters do nothing but travel all over the country, following the Dead."

"It doesn't sound good, does it?"

"Not at all."

"Now you be sure to let us know if you hear from John," she said kindly. "We'll be worried about him, and you too, until we know he's back. Please call us when you hear anything."

A stranger's compassion can be a very moving thing.

Bob had stood by listening, and by the time I hung up, his anxiety had turned to hurt, his fear to fury. John had lied to us, not once but often, and over a long period of time, to cover up his real plans. We felt betrayed—Bob particularly, as he had underwritten the purchase of the car.

We were also angry that no one at the school had notified us of John's failure to appear, even after a week had gone by. Once again I called the dean. I expected him to be on the defensive, for although neither he nor anyone else on campus knew John's whereabouts, he had seemed unconcerned, claiming that students often changed plans at the last minute and failed to appear.

"Dean Allen, this is Betsy White again, John White's mother. We've finally learned where John is. He and some friends went to a rock concert in Colorado. I suppose he intends to come back within a few days, but I really can't count on anything for certain. I assumed the college would want to know."

"Of course we're relieved," said the dean unconvincingly. "As you know, Mrs. White, I was never really worried about John's safety. I felt certain he would turn up. How did you find out where he was?"

"I got in touch with the mother of another boy who went along—Lew Grady. She knew where they were headed."

"It doesn't surprise me to hear Lew went along. I advised him last spring to drop out of school for a while because of his academic and social difficulties. I thought he needed to get his life in better order, but it sounds like he's made a bad beginning. Well, thank you for letting me know. I'll be in touch with John's faculty advisor and hall counselor, and I'll see him myself as soon as he gets back."

Bob was mouthing instructions at me: *Have him call us!*

"Dean Allen, please call us right away when you see John," I said. "I don't know how he expects to catch up in his course work. You can imagine how disappointed we are in John, and we're angry that he deceived us."

"I'm disappointed in John myself at this point. I've not been pleased with the group he's been running with, and he certainly hasn't lived up to his academic potential. Now he's not likely to get the courses he needs, as classes will be filled. I don't know what we can work out, but I'll take it up with him when I see him. I'll be back in touch with you soon. Or better still, I'll have John call you himself."

"Thank you, Dean Allen. We appreciate your help. We'll rest a great deal easier when we hear John is back."

The dean's assurances offered little comfort. We had come to realize that the chief bond among the group of kids John was traveling with was drugs, particularly LSD and other hallucinogens. It's a wretched feeling to envision your child thousands of miles away, dropping acid for the trip that may fry his brain forever.

Eventually the call came. John-with-Nine-Lives was nonchalant but touchy, very much on the defensive beneath a thin layer of cool.

"Thank God you're back, John," said Bob emotionally. I picked up the extension seconds after hearing his greeting. "Son, do you have any idea how worried we've been?"

"I don't know why," John answered offhandedly. "You both are so overprotective it makes me sick! I *am* nineteen years old, you know. I'm perfectly able to take care of myself, though you can't seem to get that through your heads."

We ignored the supercilious tone.

"John, we hadn't the slightest idea where you were," I said. "We were frightened not to know how to find you. Suppose something had happened to one of us? We couldn't even have found you to let you know. But the thing that hurt us most, son, was your dishonesty, your deceit! We trusted you, and you let us down."

"Come off it, Mom! I told you I was going camping, and I did go. I just didn't say I was going to the Rocky

Mountains instead of North Carolina. What's the difference?"

His superior tone was infuriating, but we managed to keep cool.

"All the same, John," said Bob, "we were extremely worried about you for a week and more. All we could think of when you didn't come back to school was that you were in trouble, somewhere where no one could reach you. And we had no idea where to look. Son, we were scared to death."

"You make me want to puke," said John, not troubling to be polite any longer. "You always make such a big deal out of everything. It really pisses me off. I can take care of myself, and I'm going to, no matter what you think. I just hope you two will finally decide to get off my back."

Bob's reply was surprisingly steady. "As long as your mother and I are responsible for your welfare, we can't get off your back, as you put it. It's our duty and our right to be concerned about you. I want to make it very clear to you right now how disappointed I am in your behavior. You lied to us, you deceived us, you took advantage of our good nature and our trust in you. It's going to take a long time to rebuild that trust, John."

"Well, you can go screw yourself. I'm hanging up, if that's all you have to say." And on that offensive note the conversation ended, leaving Bob and me feeling less angry than unutterably sad.

# Sick and Tired of Being
## Sick and Tired

_____ The fall of John's junior year was a disaster, beginning with his arrival after the school year had already begun. We were so out of touch with our parental powers that we could do no more than stand by and watch. His new roommate, thoroughly disgusted, soon pulled out. Living alone, John could do just as he pleased, with no one to object or complain.

Amy's absence also made a difference. She was not there to check up on him, nag, or berate him. We didn't know his friends at all, or in fact whether he had any. We had never felt more out of touch.

Then a letter came from John—a most unusual event—asking us to send him to Greece for spring term on a college-sponsored program. For Susan or Mike, it would have been a marvelous opportunity, but not for John. Horror stories of harsh drug laws and foreign prisons sprang to mind. We could see him being picked up with a bag of pot or hash in his luggage and stuck in a jail we couldn't get him out of.

When we ignored his written request, he telephoned to emphasize what a wonderful chance this was.

"You wanted Susie to go to England. Don't you want me to have the same kind of experience?"

We listened noncommittally, giving him a false signal—he believed we were considering letting him go and redoubled his efforts. He declared that going to Greece meant more to him than anything else he had ever wanted to do. This statement had a mighty familiar ring. He'd used the same line when he was working on Bob for a car.

As a dramatic performer, John was masterful. At times he almost had us convinced, until better judgment prevailed. It was a good thing the memory of the Colorado trip still rankled so sorely. After that colossal deception, we were not about to indulge John in any way whatever.

We tried to drop the subject, but he wouldn't give up. He reiterated how important it was for him to go, and later threw in the fact that Greece was all the more desirable, since his friend Thad was going to Cairo. The two planned to join forces after John's studies ended and travel together in the Middle East.

Suddenly John's single-mindedness made a lot more sense: He and Thad were planning a drug-smuggling operation! Those two long-haired, ragtag Deadheads, traveling together, would have been a magnet for every narcotics agent on the Mediterranean. Greece was out of the question!

I began to suspect that John was becoming mentally unbalanced. He seemed to have no notion how angry we were about the Colorado fiasco, or how vulnerable his drug problem would make him in the Middle East.

So in spite of John's histrionics, we stood our ground. It was time to stop pushing his chemical merry-go-round. In chemical-dependency language, we were learning to *stop enabling.*

At this tense impasse, my old college friend Sally Ann came through town. I hadn't seen her in years. We went out to lunch and talked and laughed almost nonstop throughout our delightful reunion, catching up on our families and events.

"Are you working now?" I asked.

"I guess it's work," she replied with a smile. "But I enjoy it so much, it seems more like play. I counsel families with drug problems."

"Really! How did you get into that?"

"My son is a recovering addict," she said matter-of-factly. "For years, our family life was a nightmare. Once we got the help we needed, I resolved to try to help others struggling with the same problem. That's how it started."

"How's your boy doing now?"

"Just great. He's been clean for a year and a half, and he's gone back to school."

"Sally Ann, that's wonderful. I had no idea you'd had all this trouble." A powerful impulse welled up within me, and words I hadn't planned to say came out. "Since you're telling all, I'll make a confession too. Bob and I have had a hell of a time with our boy John. It's been going on for several years now. We've concluded that drugs must be at the bottom of it."

My friend was neither pitying nor shocked, only empathetic. "Tell me about it."

So at last the floodgates were opened. I had needed to tell someone for so long that all the pain and fear and anger came pouring out in an unstoppable torrent.

Sally Ann knows her business. She nodded encouragingly and listened with a lively interest. A comment here and there let me know she'd been down this lonesome road herself. After I'd recounted the affair of the Colorado trip and John's obsession with going to Greece, she set down her coffee cup and looked directly at me in an extraordinarily compelling way.

"Betsy, there's something very important you need to know."

Her penetrating gaze threw me off-balance.

"What is it?"

"You obviously don't realize it, but John has a progressive and ultimately fatal disease."

I wasn't sure I'd heard her right.

"Say that again?"

"John has a disease called chemical dependency." She was speaking slowly, dropping each word into my consciousness like a stone into deep water. "This disease is fatal if it's not treated. John is *very* sick. It sounds like he's pretty far advanced. You and Bob must do something and do it soon! Otherwise John will die, probably within a couple of years."

What a shocking thing to be told! It took my breath away, but I have thanked God every day since for Sally Ann and her courage. In saying those deeply affective words, telling me this shocking thing, Sally Ann stretched out to save John's life as surely as if she had thrown him a life preserver in a storm-tossed sea.

And she saved my life as well. I had been chronically depressed, worn down with the effort of trying to get through to John, feeling hopeless and helpless, withdrawing from life in general. On the physical side, I was seriously overweight, with high blood pressure, chronic digestive problems, insomnia, almost constant headaches and episodes of rapid heartbeat. I had concluded that I was meant to live my life only in terms of other people's needs; and I had long ago lost my capacity for joy.

Sally Ann's words gave me back my life. She pulled me up short, gave our private monster a name, rolled back the smoke screen for the very first time. She watched my reactions as I took in what she had said.

"I want to make sure I've got this exactly right. Will you say what you just said one more time? I'll have to tell Bob, and I want to get it straight."

Her patience was infinite. "John has a disease called chemical dependency. It's a predictable, progressive disease, and if it's not arrested, it will kill him. He may also kill somebody else, in a car wreck or other accident, if he doesn't get treatment. Or he may accidentally overdose, or choke to death on his own vomit when he's passed out, or commit suicide out of shame and despair. Chemical dependency can't be cured, but its progress can be halted."

She paused to let me think.

"John will not ask for help on his own. That is probably beyond his power at the moment. It's up to you and Bob to get him to help. His disease *can* be arrested, if you act in time."

Through some mysterious inner process, I committed myself wholly to Sally Ann at that moment. I accepted every word, willing to do whatever she told me. For the first time, after all our attempts to get help, someone I knew and trusted could tell me clearly, with the ring of truth, what to do for John.

"What must I do to help him? What kind of help does he need? We've tried everything."

"He needs to be hospitalized in an inpatient treatment program for chemical dependency—not a psychiatric hospital, but a chemical-dependency program. It will be up to you and Bob to see that he goes."

My heart sank. John had done very little that Bob and I wanted him to in the past six years. The old sad, defeated feeling was coming back.

"I have no idea how to get him to do anything."

"First, get yourself a book, *I'll Quit Tomorrow* by Vernon Johnson, as soon as you can. Read every word of it. You'll know a whole lot better what you can do after that."

I was scribbling this down on a paper napkin.

"Then make a phone call—today—to this hospital in Minnesota to see how soon they can take John. Here's the number. So far as I'm concerned, it's the best treatment program in the country."

I wrote that down too.

"Once they've agreed to take John, you must use all the leverage you have to get him to treatment. Remember, he's seriously ill. It's absolutely a question of life and death. Tell him you won't send him back to school unless he goes, and mean it! Whatever you do, don't let him go to Greece. Tell him he can't live at home any more, that you won't support him, until he accepts treatment.

"Cancel his car insurance—sell the car if necessary. Enlist the help of every person who has the slightest bit of influence with him, and don't give up until you get him in that hospital. Start working on it today. Talk to the school authorities; tell them what you're planning and get their help. Get his girlfriend to help if you can."

I was trying to absorb every word of this revolutionary way of thinking, after the apathetic despair of the past.

She went on. "But use the element of surprise to your advantage. Keep your plans quiet until you're ready to move. If he gets wind of what you're doing, he will try every way possible to get out of going. It will be hard, but you must hold your ground. Don't back down. You can do it! You *have* to do it!"

My face felt flushed with excitement. I was breathing faster, feeling more alive than I had in a long while, daring to hope things really could change. It was time to act!

We hugged good-bye, and Sally Ann pressed my hands.

"Let me know how it goes," she said softly. "I'll be waiting to hear from you."

I could hardly wait to share with Bob what Sally Ann had said. That evening he called the hospital and learned they could take John very soon. Bob was already reclaiming his role as parent; hope had restored his courage and strength too.

I went to the bookstore for Vernon Johnson's book and began to read it. In *I'll Quit Tomorrow*, the disease of chemical dependency is described in exacting detail. It described John perfectly: irrational, inconsiderate behavior, low self-esteem; an endless series of calamities; hostility, deceit, denial. Every page drew a more exact likeness—everything Sally Ann had told me!

The author speaks of the *continuing series of crises* that is the hallmark of the disease. He talks about *intervention,* that the family must break through the abuser's defenses to confront him or her with reality. He tells how a family can *use the next crisis as a lever* to get the chemically dependent person to accept help. Bob read the book as soon as I finished it and was all the more resolved to get John into the hospital. At long last, we were laying a solid foundation for successful intervention. We waited and watched, readying ourselves to act when the moment came.

Two days after Sally Ann's visit, John telephoned to say he was leaving for a Grateful Dead concert in upper New York state—a round trip of more than a thousand miles. I objected flatly.

"I'm going, Mom, I'm sorry you don't like it, but this is something that's very, very important to me." *Everything* John wanted to do was very, very important to him.

"John, this is against all our better judgment. You're in college, supposed to be studying. Your grades have never been good. You can't afford this kind of frivolity. You haven't even made up what you missed by going to Colorado!"

"Hang it up, Mom." His voice was flat and unfeeling. "I've heard all your speeches before. Save your breath. I'm going. You ought to thank me for telling you my plans, instead of bitching me out."

I felt desperate. We both knew I had no hold on him.

"What if we had an emergency, John? What if Daddy or I needed you? We'd have no idea how to find you."

"Oh, that's no problem. I'll be staying with Chris," he said ingenuously, "in Syracuse. You can get me there."

"Chris who?"

"I can't remember his last name, but he's a Deadhead. Anybody there can tell you."

I hung up, despairing. *Chris, in Syracuse!* Either John didn't want us to find him, or drugs were fast destroying his mind.

No immediate course of action occurred to us after that disheartening exchange. We could have asked the highway patrol to apprehend John, though we never thought of it. It's probably just as well, for in the end, John was brought to help in a way we never could have contrived.

Fearfully, we waited. After the weekend, we phoned. John was safely back at school, and once again, he brought up the matter of Greece with a manic fervor that exceeded all that had gone before. It was total obsession. He couldn't stop talking about it, and he couldn't accept the fact that we would not let him go. This conversation also ended with the phone being hung up—by Bob.

Next morning Bob wrote John a letter. Wanting to

make sure he was not misunderstood, he labored long over his composition.

This was the final version:

Dear John,

I am certain that letting you go to Greece would be unwise in the extreme. You're tremendously vulnerable because of your drug-centered lifestyle. And as you have thoroughly deceived and blatantly disobeyed us on many occasions, your mother and I are not in the least inclined to underwrite any new frolics. Please understand that we do love you very much, and our love and concern for you are the main factors in our decision to refuse.

With my love,
Dad

This letter sent John into a frenzy that surpassed all previous ones. He called Bob at the office, interrupting his schedule of patients, to shout and abuse him. Bob merely repeated again and again, in a low firm voice, that we could not allow John to put himself at such risk.

John raged for more than twenty minutes, spouted obscenities, poured out fiendish depths of hatred Bob had never dreamed his soul could harbor. The tirade ended at last when Bob cut in, "Son, it's final. I'm sorry," and hung up.

Bob knew when he wrote the letter that John would indulge in a temper fit, but he was not prepared for such a torrent of hostility and vituperation. The ragings on the phone sounded like those of a madman.

As for John, he was sobered by this event. He realized he had been completely out of control and, still trembling, sought out Dr. Callahan, a favorite professor. For nearly an hour he poured out his pain and frustration to that gracious man, who patiently heard him out. He let John know he thought he was out of line, yet indicated his concern and desire to help. He probably kept John from going over the brink that afternoon.

After his talk with Dr. Callahan, John put in a call to Susan and poured out his agitation for another hour. The moment their conversation ended, she called us. Here was another old pattern: the election of Susan as go-between.

"Mom, I just got through talking to John."

I motioned to Bob to pick up the extension phone.

"I'm *really* worried about him this time." Her voice trembled. "It's not like the other times, the way he used to be at school. Something has changed. He sounds like he's about to go crazy. The way he was talking about the Grateful Dead, he sounded like a religious fanatic.

"I told him he was talking like a Moonie. He was telling me about wanting to become a vegetarian, not wanting to have to eat anything that was alive, wanting to live like the Deadheads, not caring anything about property or money.

"That was only part of what he said. There was a lot about God and enlightenment, but none of it made any sense. I got really scared listening to him. I told him he was scaring me. I think you'd better go see about him just as soon as you can. Don't wait any longer." Her voice caught and wavered. "Can you go tonight?"

Bob was trying to understand. "Can you believe all this came about just because I wrote John that he couldn't go to Greece? If that's the case, you're right, Susie. John is in a bad way. He sounded crazy when he called me today too."

John *was* nearing the outer limits of rationality, but none of us sensed that he had reached the brutal edge.

I tried to reassure Susie. "Thanks for calling, honey. We're not going to sit back and do nothing. Try not to worry. We'll let you know what happens. One of us will go down to see John. We're going to try to get him into a hospital for drug treatment."

"I sure am glad to hear you say that." She gave a great sigh of relief. "Just please don't wait too long. I love John, and I'm scared to death for him."

We calculated that John's frenzy over Bob's letter must have lasted seven or eight hours—far too long for somebody who couldn't take no for an answer.

We decided I should go to John. As the recent object of his fury, Bob might seem too threatening, and John was usually more comfortable with me. An hour before midnight, I was ready to get in the car and start for Chambers. A wiser Bob persuaded me to wait until morning.

Up to this point Mike had not been involved in the matter, though he had heard us talking to Susan. As usual, we had pretty well overlooked him, and he preferred to stay clear of family conflicts.

But this time I asked his opinion:

"Mike, I'm planning to drive to Chambers early in the morning to see John and try to get him into a hospital for treatment of his drug problem. What do you think?"

Mike's immediate and fervent answer brought tears to my eyes. "Go for it, Mom!"

That was all the encouragement I needed. Mike cared too, even though he took great pains most of the time to conceal the fact. His own experimentation with alcohol and other drugs kept him from condemning John, but he recognized how sick John was at this point and really wanted him to get help.

By 4:00 in the morning, I was up and on my way. I shared the road with a few truckers under the dark sky, but my thoughts were my chief companions on that unforgettable journey. I asked God to make John's heart ready and give me the right words to say. As the coral streaks of dawn gradually appeared in the sky, I knew I was not alone in going to do what I had been afraid to do for so long. A Higher Power was upholding me, along with the loving concern of Mike, Susan, and Bob. I was the only one making the trip, but all of us were going.

As the darkness retreated I hummed and sang. Anxiety had melted away in the earliest moments of the journey; now there was only confidence and faith. Everything was falling into place. I was strangely unconcerned about the outcome, knowing all would be well.

I drove through the college gates as early-rising students made their way to 8:00 classes. A sunny fall day was unfolding, every yellow and scarlet leaf luminous against the sky. Such a day was bound to be a good omen.

I found John's dorm and room, and knocked on the door. I heard no answer, so I opened it and went in. The sight that greeted me was daunting, to say the least. The floor was covered with dirty clothes, beer cans, ashtrays full of butts. A bong sat in the middle of the room, its spilled water soaking into the filthy rug.

John was asleep in the top bunk in a greasy sleeping bag, on a bare mattress. His hair was lank and dirty, his face pasty, and he had a couple of days' stubble on his chin. The room was hung with Grateful Dead posters; a ragged American flag was suspended from the ceiling. The pervasive odor was disgusting—a combination of stale beer, the sickly sweetness of pot, dirty socks, accumulated cigarette ashes, and unwashed bodies.

John raised his head and opened his puffy eyes.

"Hello, son."

"Mom! What are you doing here?" Hampered in his efforts to get up by lack of pajamas, he seemed glad to see me nevertheless. "Turn around for a minute, will you, so I can get up."

I did as he asked and heard him climb down from the bunk.

"Okay, I'm decent now. You can turn around. Now, what did you say you were doing here?" He had hastily pulled on a ragged pair of jeans.

I hadn't known what I would say, but the words came unbidden.

"I thought you were in trouble, son. I came to see if I could help."

That was apparently the message John wanted to hear, for his eyes gleamed with tears and he enfolded me in a powerful embrace. All along, my journey had seemed appropriate and right; now I knew it was so. Through a process I did not understand, a change had taken place in John. I was not going to have to do the whole job by myself. He was participating, responding, helping! As John held me, he trembled, and when we drew apart I saw that he was too moved to speak. I broke the tension.

"I thought I'd spend the day with you, if that suits you. What classes do you have this morning?"

It took him a few moments to get his brain in gear. "Well, I have a 9:00, and then I'm free for the day."

"Fine! After your class, we'll get some breakfast. Then we'll have the rest of the day to spend together in the city. We'll do whatever you'd like. This is your day."

"Sounds good, Mom." John was regaining his poise and habitual superficiality. "Why don't you go over the Union and get yourself a cup of coffee? I'll come after class." He realized I couldn't wait in that room!

"See you in a little while, then," I said and closed the door behind me. The campus was waking up. Students were making their way to the cafeteria, the post office, the library. Considering the scene I had just left, I felt remarkably happy. The Student Union was buzzing with chatter—a throng of fresh young faces, as yet reflecting few of the scars life leaves behind in its passing. One or two glum ones mirrored their owners' hangovers, and there were a couple of puffy-faced, lank-haired types like John, but by and large, it was a cheerful, vivacious group. I sipped my coffee slowly; I enjoyed being surrounded by so much vitality.

Outside the window, the autumn leaves reminded me of the sadness we'd been living with, our fears for John's survival, our longing for him to be like these bright young people. I had plenty to think about as I waited.

At length, I spotted my boy striding cheerfully along. However raunchy his clothes and grooming, the look on his face was a happy one. Perhaps it really was going to be all right! The Chinese have a saying—"When the pupil is ready, the teacher appears." Could it be that John was finally ready?

He was still all smiles when he reached my table.

"Hi, Mom."

"How did your class go?"

"Oh, okay. I'm through for the day now. We can do whatever you want."

"We have all day. Why don't you get yourself a good big breakfast for starters?"

"That sounds great to me, if you don't mind waiting. And, uh, Mom, by the way, I'm a little broke. Could you let me have enough money to eat on?"

I handed him a $5 bill without comment. John received his allowance once a month. One week was gone, and his whole allowance with it.

He stoked up with a big breakfast—eggs, bacon,

several pieces of toast, juice, and milk, then flashed one of his most engaging smiles.

"Well, Mom, I'm ready if you are."

We walked along under the brilliant trees to the parking lot. John was wearing the skeletal remains of tennis shoes—rubber soles and laces. He had wrapped duct tape around the few remaining shreds of canvas to hold them together.

"Son, have you any other shoes?" I tried to keep my tone neutral.

"Sorry, Mom, these are all I have. I had some good ones earlier in the year, but I can't seem to find them." Shoes, jackets, sunglasses—so many of his clothes and belongings regularly disintegrated or mysteriously disappeared. I was used to it.

"First of all, let's find you a decent pair of shoes. It'll be turning cold soon. You'll need something warmer. Then we can have lunch somewhere nice and decide what else we want to do."

John was agreeable. We were driving toward the city by then. He turned the conversation to his obsession, going to Greece.

"I blew my cool yesterday when I called Dad," he began diplomatically. "I'm sorry about that. But this thing of going to Greece is really important to me. I don't think either of you has any idea how important it is. Will you talk to Dad again and see if you can get him to let me go? It matters more to me right now than anything else in the world." Had I been a novice at these exchanges, I might have agreed that of course he should be allowed to go. But I'd heard all John's speeches before.

Something was telling me this was the opening I had been waiting for. I inhaled deeply and took the plunge.

"John, it's not negotiable. Daddy and I simply cannot let

you go to Greece, as things stand now. Your problem makes it impossible."

No reply, but no resistance either.

"Frankly, John," I went on boldly, "you're going to find a lot of things impossible until you come to terms with your basic problem."

I had said it. I was ready for any consequences. He might fling open the door and throw himself onto the highway, or curse and scream at me, or simply face me with a silent, malevolent stare.

The suspense lasted only a few seconds. A calm and guileless expression playing over his face, he asked, "Do you mean drugs?"

"Yes, son, I do mean drugs." I crossed my fingers and prayed.

"What do you think I ought to do about it?"

The battle was over. There might be a few skirmishes along the way, but the critical engagement was won. I contained my joy, afraid that any show of feeling might cost me the ground I had gained.

"I came here with a plan to propose. Your dad and I want you to take medical leave from school and check yourself into a hospital for a drug treatment program."

Still no resistance. I could scarcely believe it.

"Well, if you think that's what I need to do, I'm willing to go," he said, utterly humble. "But I don't know of a place."

My answer was ready. "Dad has made arrangements with a hospital in Minnesota. A friend of mine told me about it; her son went there. She says it's the most wonderful place imaginable, and her boy has been straight for well over a year since his treatment."

"How long would I have to stay?"

"The treatment program lasts a month. You'll only have

to miss a few months of school. That's not much, considering the importance of this thing for the rest of your life. I feel sure we can work out the details."

We reached a department store, and I parked the car.

"All right, Mom. I'll go."

It had all been so simple! John seemed relieved, even thankful. What had brought him to this? Clearly, he had been waiting for someone to get him over the last hurdle—the one he could not clear by himself, no matter how much he realized he needed to make the effort.

I took his hand. He stared straight ahead, unwilling to risk a glance at me.

"Son, I'm as sure as I've ever been of anything that you've made the best decision of your life. I'm proud of your courage, and I don't think you'll ever regret your choice."

The rest of that day is a rosy haze in my mind. We bought the shoes. We had lunch at a little Italian place. We stopped by a drugstore for shampoo, razor blades, deodorant.

Suddenly I felt extremely tired. My supply of adrenaline had run out. Lack of sleep the night before and the day's emotional strains were starting to take their toll.

"You know, John, I think I'll check into the college guesthouse and stay overnight. I'm really too tired to drive home today."

"Fine, Mom. Do you think we could go out to dinner tonight?"

"I'd love it. You choose the place."

A long and untroubled nap followed by a refreshing bath worked wonders. John came to meet me just as dusk fell, and we set off for the city again, this time in a vastly different frame of mind. John's favorite Mexican restaurant was crowded and cheerful, redolent with appetizing aromas. We set ourselves up to a beer. I didn't understand that alcohol was as much of a problem for John as other drugs, but in view of the morning's decision, one more beer couldn't matter much.

He looked fine, sitting across the table from me, clean and freshly shaven, his hair shining. The white shirt reflected candlelight toward his face, emphasizing the fineness of his features. His excesses had not ruined his looks. His expression showed a calm I had despaired of ever seeing again.

"Mom, I'm really enjoying having dinner with you," he said almost shyly. "I'm glad you stayed."

"I'm glad I did too. We deserve a little celebration. I haven't felt this happy for a long time."

When the food came, John put it away as though he hadn't eaten a good meal in weeks.

"When was the last time you had a meal away from school?"

"Never, this term. I never have enough money."

I didn't need to ask why.

"I went around campus to see all my friends this afternoon," he confided around a mouthful of enchilada. "I told them what I'm going to do."

"Did you! How did they react?"

"They all were really glad to hear it. They congratulated me and told me they were happy for me. A couple of girls hugged me. I guess they must think I need to go."

If John had made his plans common knowledge, he evidently was really committed.

"I'll write Amy about it tonight," he went on. "I know she'll be happy. She's been worried about me for a long time."

When I dropped John at his dorm, we both were more at peace than we'd been in years. Some anxious times lay ahead, but the die was cast. My sleep that night was long, deep, and restorative.

Next morning we called on Dean Allen to get permission for John's leave of absence. The dean was wary, not knowing what was afoot, but our faces told him the news was good.

"Dean Allen, John wants to take a medical leave from school to undergo treatment for his drug problem," I said. "The treatment takes a month. He'll be at home with us for two months, then come back to school for the next quarter, if you agree."

"That's splendid news." The dean was visibly relieved. "I'm completely behind you—that is, provided it's an inpatient program. John can certainly take a medical leave under those circumstances. Where is the hospital?"

"It's in Minnesota. We're told it's one of the best."

Dean Allen stood up and extended his hand.

"Well, son, I wish you nothing but good. I hope this puts you where you need to be."

"I hope so too," said John, shaking the dean's hand.

"Will you leave before exams?"

"No sir, I don't want to lose my credits for this quarter. It's just a month more. After that I'll go home, and then on to Minnesota, I guess."

"I'll be thinking about you," said the dean.

John walked me to the car and stood watching as I drove through the front gate.

# CHAPTER NINE

# The Last Mile Is the Longest

_____*I* had concentrated so hard on arranging things for John, I'd completely forgotten the rest of the family. At the first highway interchange, I located a phone booth.

Bob's anxiety carried plainly across the miles.

"Bad news or good news?"

"Nothing but good. John's agreed to go for treatment as soon as his exams are over."

"Thank God! *Thank God!* Did you have a hard time persuading him? How did he take it?"

"You can't imagine how easy it was. He was gentle as a lamb, appreciated my coming, listened to what I had to say. When I suggested going for treatment, he agreed on the spot. Don't ask me what brought about the change. It's a mystery. I'm just accepting it gratefully. Apparently I showed up at the critical moment, when he was finally ready to accept help." I laughed. "Maybe The Force was with us!"

Bob laughed too, reveling in the good news. "I just can't believe it! What a wonderful relief! I'll give Susie a call, and you can tell Mike when you get home.

"After you left, he told me he realized last summer that

John was going downhill fast. Do you know, that scoundrel knew all about John's plans to go to Colorado and never said a word! We obviously have a lot of things to work on."

On my way home I had ample time to reflect on the amazing turnaround in our situation. After nearly five years of chaos, John had turned this all-important corner. Why now?

I thought about all the times I had prayed so desperately for a change, walking the floor during those long nights: *Dear God, please make John stop drinking. I know it's within your power, Lord. Help him leave drugs alone. Show him a better way. Change him.* The last two words echoed through my memories like a broken record: *Change him. Change him. Change him.*

That was it! All the time I was praying so hard for John to be changed, I had remained blind to my *own* desperate need to change! As long as I reacted to his behavior with anger, resentment, and resistance, he was forced to fight me, as well as his own dependency. When I surrendered to a new way of thinking, everything else—including John—changed in response. When I entered his room at Chambers, I had approached him, for the first time in years, without accusing or judging: "I thought you were in trouble, son. I came to see if I could help."

God requires our participation in bringing about change. When we pray for a healthy change in the life of a person we love, we must be willing to accept change in ourselves as well. No matter how much I love another person, I cannot change that person. I can only change myself. If I become utterly willing to surrender my own agenda and will to God's greater plan and will, then and only then can He use me to touch someone else.

The next couple of weeks were busy ones. We bought

clothes suitable for Minnesota, arranged plane tickets, read the literature the hospital sent. A staff counselor phoned us for help in accumulating a history.

"We need some idea of what living with John has been like for you and your family."

I laughed ruefully. "How much time do you have?"

"Well, just make a start, and when I've heard enough I'll let you know."

Twenty minutes later I was just getting warmed up, but he interrupted.

"Okay, I get the picture. It sounds like a classic story of chemical dependency, but I can't make a final judgment yet. John will spend his first few days here in detox and observation. After that, our evaluation team will determine whether he really is chemically dependent and should stay for treatment. If not, he can be discharged home."

"Will you risk an educated guess?"

"My guess is he'll have to stay. You and your family should probably plan to come for Family Week. If he doesn't need to stay, you can always cancel out."

"I imagine I'll be the only family member coming. My husband has a busy practice. He can't take time off unless it's absolutely essential, and I'm sure our other son won't want to give up his Christmas holidays."

His response was emphatic: "Everyone who can come should come. We operate on the principle that chemical dependency is a family illness. The whole family needs help with making changes and understanding John's disease. It's much easier if you do it together, and John's going to need all the emotional support you can give him. When we've completed his evaluation I'll see that you receive the information on Family Week. Can we expect to see all of you then?"

"If you say so, we'll be there."

Even though our phone bill had approached the national debt, I wanted to make one more call.

"Sally Ann? This is Betsy."

"Tell me quick!"

"Great news! John's agreed to go for treatment."

"Fantastic! You did good, babe! Was it hard to talk him into going?"

"Not at all. I guess he knew he needed help."

"You were mighty lucky. It's not usually that simple. When does he leave?"

"In a few weeks, after his exams."

"Too bad you couldn't have put him on the plane the same day. It's a big risk, waiting. Any party could be his last, especially if he's doing acid or coke. And the longer the delay, the more likely he'll be to try to back out."

"We don't think he's doing anything besides pot and alcohol, and I have a strong feeling he's not going to back out."

"Okay, but don't be overconfident. As the time draws near, he'll get scared. You have to remember he's in love with his drugs. They're his best friend, the thing that's holding his life together. He'll be afraid treatment will destroy his identity, that once the drugs are gone, there won't be anything left of John. He'll think he's going to be brainwashed."

"What should we do?"

"Hang tough. Keep your hand in his back. Don't let him wiggle out of going. Don't even let him know you admit the possibility. You've come so far now, you have to make it all the way. Don't forget—treatment means saving his life. Keep telling yourself that. And keep telling him, too."

"I will. Thanks for the encouragement."

"Oh, there is one thing that may help ease his fears. Give him the phone number and have him call the hospital himself. By making that contact, he'll be taking some initiative for his own recovery. Once he talks to a counselor there, he'll sense their concern and understanding. You can't imagine it yet, but it's the most therapeutic, cleansing, healing environment possible— not just for John, but for the whole family. It's going to be one of the best things that's ever happened to you. Get John to call. After that, he'll feel a lot better."

"Thanks, Sal. I don't know what we would have done without you."

"I just happened to be in the right place at the right time. You can thank me by helping some other family get the help they need. That's all the thanks I want."

John phoned the hospital willingly; when he reported on the call, relief was audible in his voice.

"I talked to a really nice guy out there named Sam. I could tell he understood. I felt totally comfortable talking to him about my problem. He's been through treatment himself, so he knew where I was coming from."

"Do you feel okay about going?"

"I was feeling okay about it to start with, but since I've talked to this guy, I feel even better. In fact, I'm kind of looking forward to it."

"Well, all systems are go at this end. We've got your plane ticket and clothes ready."

"Who's flying out there with me, you or Dad?"

"Nobody. You're going by yourself."

"Aren't you afraid I'll split?"

"I can't imagine you'd let yourself and everybody else down by backing out. You're a big guy. I think you'll do what you have to do."

"Well, thanks, Mom. I'm glad you trust me."

A very real danger was the likelihood that John would

indulge in one last tremendous blow-out. His Deadhead friends were having a big Halloween party.

"I think we should tell him he can't go," said Bob.

"How do you propose to make it stick?"

"Just tell him he can't go. That's all there is to it."

"Bob, get serious. John's only agreed to go to treatment. He hasn't had a complete personality change! You know he'll go to this party if he wants to, no matter what we say. We'll just have to trust the strength of his commitment."

"I hope you're right. Everything's gone so well so far, I'd hate to blow it now."

When John finally made it home, he was pretty well burned out. The night before, he had partied until the sun came up, crashed, then slept until late afternoon. He didn't arrive home until 10:30 that night. Although he had a couple of beers and several empties in the car with him, he had eaten nothing and had no money. I was reminded of an injured dog, coming home to lick its wounds under the back porch. Too beat even to eat a bowl of soup, he fell into bed and slept for fourteen straight hours. Bob and I rested almost as soundly, knowing our boy was home and the nightmare was nearly over.

It came out during Family Week that John took the last of fifty acid trips at that Halloween party. The toll drugs were taking on his body and mind was all too evident. Considering the shape he was in, I was amazed that he'd managed to stay in school.

The state of his nerves was not good. When I asked him to help with the dishes, he exploded in a fit of temper.

He described various physical feelings: "First I feel hot all over and then cold." At another time: "I feel as if I have a fever. I can't tell whether I'm hot or cold." Later: "I don't know what's the matter with me. I just feel sick in general." He had a persistent dry cough and frequently complained of chest pain. Often he was pale, perspiring, jittery, restless.

In reality, we were dealing with withdrawal symptoms. When I discovered that food would alleviate his discomfort, I kept a ready supply of snacks and treats on hand and offered them when the distress began to appear. After a couple of toaster tarts, he would begin to feel better.

Several times during John's two weeks at home, he asked one of us for money. We had agreed that no one should let him have any. If he wanted gas, we told him to charge it. If he wanted anything else, one of us went along and bought it. On one occasion, when he looked particularly wretched, I did buy him a pack of cigarettes; it seemed a small enough kindness.

With time on his hands, John often hung around one or another family member, wanting to talk. He lingered in the kitchen one day, watching me cut up vegetables for stew. I felt bold enough to ask him a big question, trying to make it sound ordinary.

"What drugs have you used, son, besides pot? I'm sure they'll want to know at the hospital."

He shrugged. "You name it."

"Well, I know about pot. What about cocaine? Have you tried that? Have you ever taken LSD?"

"A couple of times." He was getting edgy now.

"How many times?"

"I don't know. A few." He had probably said as much as he was going to, but I pressed my luck.

"Well, five times? Ten? More than ten?"

"Yeah, I guess so." He would say no more.

It was naive to expect John to level with me; alcoholics and addicts always minimize or deny their use, even in the face of irrefutable evidence. "A couple of beers" may mean two six-packs. "One or two joints" may mean getting high three or four times a day. And of course "a drink" can be anything—an iced-tea glass full of straight vodka, for example! Whatever family members know about an addict's choice of drugs and the amount used is usually only the tip of the iceberg. During Family Week, when we learned how much John was actually using, we were flabbergasted. If you know a little, there's probably ten times more to be known.

"I don't plan to stop using drugs, or alcohol either," John said suddenly. "I'm really just going to the hospital so I can stop smoking. I figure they can teach me to drink and do drugs in moderation. But I do need to stop smoking."

Talk about delusional thinking! It didn't really matter to me what John said at this point, as long as he actually entered that treatment program. That was all-important! We would leave attitude adjustment up to the treatment-center staff.

"If that's what you want, I hope you can accomplish it."

"I can, I'm sure. I can handle everything, if I want to. It's just that I don't always want to."

Another day I took a new tack.

"John, what about Amy? Does she do drugs?"

"About as much as you use alcohol," he answered testily. I let that slide too, but I wondered: Would he need to change his whole pattern of social life, including his relationship with Amy? But that also could be decided later.

John was eager to see Amy again. She was returning from abroad around the end of his stay in treatment. A postcard with a European postmark brought her reply to his letter telling of his decision to get help:

"*Thrilled* to hear your wonderful news! I know it will be a good thing for you, and maybe it will be good for us too. Can't wait to see you when I get back! So much to tell! All my love, Amy."

John still listened to his Grateful Dead tapes for long periods of time, particularly when he felt anxious or sad. He planned to take them along to the hospital.

"Surely you can get along without them for a month." I thought he would do well to leave this reminder of the "high life" behind.

"No way! I'm taking them! Anyway," he said, flashing a disarming smile, "I'll probably find a lot of my Deadhead brothers and sisters up there to keep me company!" He proved to be an accurate prophet.

The afternoon before John left I was doing his laundry. He opened the dryer to check on my progress and let out a furious bellow:

"Goddammit, what have you done to my tie-dye shirts?"

It was Hostile John again, but this time I stood my ground.

"Washed and dried them," I said staunchly. "If you don't like the way I'm doing it, get your butt in here and do it yourself." I marched out of the laundry room and up the stairs.

He sought me out shortly to apologize.

"I'm sorry, Mom. I don't know what came over me. I appreciate your trying to help. I know I overreacted."

"Okay, John. I'll forget it this time."

I helped him carry the clean clothes to his room and we started to pack. In the midst of the process, he lay back dispiritedly on the bed and stared moodily at the ceiling.

"Mom, I've changed my mind about the hospital. I don't think I want to go after all."

Thanks to Sally Ann, I was prepared. I kept my tone and manner briskly unsympathetic.

"You may feel that way right this minute, but those are only transitory feelings. Once you get there, you'll feel *much* better." Addicts are superaware of the attitudes of those around them. John perceived instantly that I was fresh out of wimpiness. He said no more and we went on packing.

At last the big day came. It rained all morning and the hours dragged by. Bob told John good-bye and left for work, leaving me to see him off. The drive to the airport took forever, and it seemed an eternity before the flight was announced. In the boarding area, I asked John if he were afraid of the experience ahead.

"Not really. I guess I'm more or less relieved. I know it's something I've been needing to do for a long time."

We sat gazing out at the runway in a companionable silence. The day was grey and dreary, the clouds oppressively low. John's plane taxied slowly toward us from the end of the field. As it pulled up before our gate, a radiant, unexpected shaft of sunshine penetrated the clouds, illuminating everything with a clean and purifying light. It was as though our smoke screen had been lifted for a moment. And then the clouds lowered once again and all was gray.

Final boarding for John's flight was called. He stood up and enfolded me in a bear hug, the twin of the one he'd given me when I showed up at Chambers. His eyes moist and shining, he gazed earnestly into my face, strong hands gripping my shoulders.

"You take care of yourself, Mom, you hear?"

I nodded, too full of emotion to reply. He picked up his bag and made his way through the gate. As he mounted the steps of the plane, he turned for one final wave before he disappeared inside. He was truly on his way.

Several hours later he phoned from the hospital.

"Well, I made it!" His voice sounded almost jubilant, cheerful, and relaxed. "They're having a blizzard here, but I managed all right. Everybody here at the hospital is just as nice as can be. You don't need to worry about me. I'll be fine."

John had turned the biggest corner of his life, ready to be healed, accepting the main chance without flinching. He had gratefully placed his life in someone else's hands at last, after so many years of mismanagement and waste.

The next news came by postcard. It's still my favorite piece of literature:

Dear Family,

Everything's going real well and looking nothing but optimistic. I'm doing fine and miss and love you all. I'd rather tell you what's going on here when you come for Family Week. This experience is going to be good for our relationships with each other, as well as my relationship between me and myself. I just want to let you know that I love and miss you all. I'll see you soon.

Much love,

John

They were the sweetest words Bob and I had ever read. We stuck the card up on the refrigerator door and read it every day.

Mike was as pleased as we were. "I think John's going to make it," he told us with a satisfied grin.

Later there were phone calls, always cheerful, always

encouraging. We could scarcely believe the change in his voice. At home he had seemed sick, tentative, depressed. Once he reached the hospital, he began to reclaim his life, his health and wholeness, giving all his energies to the task. It was glorious, wonderful, marvelous—almost too good to believe.

And yet I feel sad and somewhat apologetic after writing those last few words, because so many families have not had a happy ending to their agonies. It is tragically true that some chemically dependent individuals just simply do not get well. Many parents are never privileged to hear the beautiful words we heard as John began to recover. Our family's pain was considerable, but many families of addicts suffer far more and far longer than we did. All I can say is that my heart goes out to all such families, and I pray that everyone whose life is blighted by addiction may finally be brought to healing.

We who have emerged from the darkness must continue to go back inside to lead our fellow sufferers out into the light. Not everyone will make it, but with our help and God's, many thousands will.

We made our plans to attend Family Week. Bob blocked off the whole week on his office schedule. At first Mike balked.

"John's the druggie, not me! I don't see why I should have to spend my whole Christmas vacation with a bunch of potheads in a hospital! You can forget it! I'm not going."

I called on Sally Ann for help.

"Make him go," she said at once. "When we went for our boy's Family Week, our daughter was the most important one there. She knew things about him that none of the rest of us knew. Having her there made a critical difference. You can make Mike go. Just tell him he has to."

Sally Ann's gumption and backbone were always tonic for me. Each time I relapsed into victimhood, the sound of her voice jacked me up and got me back on track.

"Mike, how would you feel about Family Week if your being there was the one thing that saved John's life? Would you go then?"

"Yeah, I'd go then. But is that true?"

"Yes, I think it probably is. You know more about him than anybody else, and you can help him face up to some things he might dodge if just Dad and I went. Your being there may make all the difference."

"Okay, I'll go, if it's really that important."

We didn't ask Susan to go because of her obligations of graduate school, part-time job, and new marriage. Looking back on that decision, I see it as a mistake. She was willing and ready to go; as the One-Still-in-Control, *I* decided she needn't. But it has taken Susan longer than the rest of us to understand all the ramifications of our family's dysfunction and John's illness. She still occasionally relapses into thinking she is responsible for her brother's disease—that he became an addict because she was mean to him when he was little! The truth is far simpler. John became an addict because he was genetically disposed to become one.

Susie also needed to deal with a lot of old pain and anger, and she could have benefited from learning about her role as the Hero in our dysfunctional family system. During Family Week, she could have worked her way through the lingering guilt, to discover that she is responsible for no one but herself—at least as far as feelings are concerned.

*Everyone who has an opportunity to participate in*

*family therapy should jump at the chance.* It was the best thing that ever happened to the three of us who did go.

As our time to leave drew near, Bob and I were anxious and even depressed, which was strange considering how happy we were. I don't know why this happens, but I've heard other families report the same thing. Merely acknowledging our feelings to one another helped, and we forged ahead.

As the plane skimmed over the snow-covered prairie, our excitement mounted. We took a cab straight to the hospital and found John in his room, asleep. He was pale, but looked peaceful and healthy. Bob woke him gently. John seemed uneasy at first, as though frightened of having to face us. Mike tried to put him at ease with an invitation; he had just been skiing for the first time and loved it.

"When you get home, John, you'll have to go skiing with me and my friends." Good old Mike was reaching out to John by offering to share something he considered extra special. To our surprise, John turned him down.

"Thanks for asking, Mike, but I don't think I can go. You guys might be drinking and getting high, and I can't participate. I have to center my social life in other ways." We were impressed. After making this statement, he seemed more relaxed and eager to share his experiences.

But Bob wondered about his reply. "John, I know you have a problem with pot and other drugs. But you don't have an alcohol problem, do you?"

Ignorant about John's disease of chemical dependency, like most physicians, Bob had failed to recognize alcohol as America's number-one drug.

"I'm a chemically dependent person, Dad," John told him. "Marijuana is my drug of preference. Although I'm not physically addicted to marijuana, I *am* addicted to the experience of getting high. If I give up pot and switch to alcohol, I'll just be changing my drug of preference. A chemically dependent person can't use any mind-altering substances."

Hearing John speak about his disease in such a serious and understanding way was profoundly moving. In order for him to have gained such a deep understanding in only three weeks, his heart must have been truly open and ready to be healed.

"I have to say good-bye for now," he told us, glancing at his watch. "I have to go to an A.A. meeting. But I'll see you tomorrow."

We hugged and kissed, confident that we all were going to make it together.

# CHAPTER TEN

# Learning to Live with It
## —And Without It

_____ Once over the anxious hurdle of meeting John, we could relax and take Family Week as an opportunity rather than a duty. The treatment-program rules prohibited further direct contact with the patient until midweek. We needed to learn the skills of healthy family communication before we could be brought together again. Glimpses of him at lectures and in the cafeteria reassured us; he was generally smiling and serene.

The five days of Family Week were full. Each day we heard two lectures, although that's a boring name for experiences that were invariably stimulating and exciting. A variety of topics was covered:

An Overview of Chemical Dependency
Family Response to the Illness
Feelings and Defenses
Spiritual Aspects of the Program
Change
Communications
Self-awareness

What Happens After Treatment
Going Home [a scary one!]
Recovery

Many chemical-dependency counselors are recovering addicts themselves, so their remarks carry the same ring of earned wisdom I had heard from Sally Ann. A good counselor excels in compassion and honesty. These people made no attempt to conceal their human imperfections, to impress, threaten, or overpower us. As utterly real human beings, they stood up before us, shared a little of their own journeys with wit and humor, and helped us forge an understanding of the challenge we were up against.

We learned that chemical dependency is classified as a disease by the American Medical Association, can be described in medical and physiological terms, and has a definable onset and predictable outcome. Untreated, it is uniformly fatal.

Sally Ann had already spelled out some possible outcomes of untreated chemical dependency. Her list was now expanded:

—Death by automobile accident, as driver or victim (the drunk who lies down on the railroad tracks or passes out in the middle of the highway)
—Overdose (accidental or intentional)
—Alcohol poisoning (the fraternity pledge found dead after a night of monumental drinking)
—Suicide grounded in shame and despair
—Death by fire (passing out while a cigarette continues to burn, or from free-basing)
—Brain damage from chronic alcohol intoxication or hallucinogens (the "burn-out" or "waste case")

—Cardiac arrest (usually from cocaine, sometimes from other drugs)

—Fatal hemorrhaging from esophageal blood vessels

—Delirium tremens (D.T.s) or alcoholic seizures

—Violent death linked to infringement of the drug-commerce code

Denial is an astonishing phenomenon. Even though my own brother was found dead in a hotel room, the victim of a lethal combination of whiskey and barbiturates (the latter prescribed by a well-meaning but ignorant physician), I had never thought that any such event might happen to John.

Many licit but powerful mind-altering substances are prescribed by physicians: antidepressants, tranquilizers, sleeping pills, diet pills, sedatives. Government-regulated alcohol, if used by adults according to state laws, is a licit chemical—a depressant, although it's usually thought of as a stimulant. Used by minors, however, alcohol is an illicit chemical. Myriad other illicit chemicals or street drugs are also readily available: marijuana, hash, cocaine in all its forms, heroin, uppers and downers (which may be black-market licit drugs), hallucinogens of many kinds, and bootleg alcohol. Any and all of these psychoactive drugs can produce addiction.

Addiction is not a condition of dependency upon any specific substance. Rather, it is the all-consuming desire for the mood change produced by such substances. Most addicts have a particular drug of preference—pot, cocaine, LSD, straight gin, peach wine, even vanilla extract or cough syrup. If the preferred drug is unavailable, the chemically dependent person uses any available substitute to produce the desired high. Thus alcoholism and drug addiction are really two faces of the same disease. The difference in labels arises from the individual's preferred chemical. We finally understood that *all* mind-altering chemicals were off-limits for John.

There is no doubt that we live in a chemical culture. Spend a week sometime taking note of TV commercials and printed ads that promote mind-altering chemicals; the volume will astonish you. "Riunite on ice—it's nice!" "It's Miller time!" "Go for the gusto!" "It's the pain medication prescribed by leading physicians." "I haven't got time for the pain!"

The message is twofold: We deserve to feel good all the time, and chemicals are the quickest way to achieve that good feeling. Surrounded by such seductive messages, a youngster caught up in the emotional turmoil of adolescence may quite naturally crave those good feelings in place of his or her uncomfortable ones.

When a friend says, "Try some of this—it's fantastic!" the invitation may be too alluring to refuse. And at first, it *is* fantastic. A new user generally loves the feeling of euphoria or well-being. If the first experience is not up to expectations, the neophyte may use several more times until the anticipated good feelings are achieved, actually practicing getting high by repetition.

With continued use, however, the euphoria becomes harder to obtain and is less pronounced. And after the drug's initial euphoric effects wear off, counteractive negative feelings set in. The user must then resort to the chemical more frequently and in larger doses to produce the high, which is replaced in its turn by a "down," and so on, ad infinitum. Vernon Johnson's book *I'll Quit Tomorrow* describes the process in eloquent detail. The grim cycle of addiction has begun.

We learned that chemical dependency is a "feeling" disorder. Mind-altering chemicals distort the addict's emotional state, and in response to the addict's destructive behavior, everyone else in the family begins to conceal true feelings and suppress, or "stuff," unpleasant emotions. These buried emotions accumulate more and more power until, like a time bomb, they are ready to go off at any moment.

Chemical dependency is indeed a family illness. Family members and friends are invariably drawn into the cycle and experience many of the same effects of the illness as the addict. Frustration, anger, hostility, depression—John was chronically in the grip of all these. In time, the rest of our family caught the same emotions. And none of us understood healthy ways of handling them. Recovery is necessary for *all* family members, not just the chemically dependent one.

We learned about the progressive effects of the disease of addiction. Specialists in chemical dependency recognize that addiction affects the family emotionally, intellectually, physically, and spiritually. Over time, more and more losses occur in all these areas. John's abandonment of church life after leaving home was one such loss. His diminishing physical condition was another. His intellectual powers were on the decline, as he had realized when one of his professors handed back a term paper with a terse comment: "F—Not the topic assigned." And the emotional life of our whole family had been an ever-worsening mess for years.

The family can be misled by the user's periodic attempts to cut down or stop using. John had always been careful how much he drank at home. Offered a beer, a glass of wine, or a highball in our company, he often declined or, if he did accept, rarely finished it. Our failure to see him as alcoholic was tied to what we observed. And we never saw him in the act of using drugs, although we saw the *results* many times.

In a social context with his peers, it was a different story. During Family Week he told us that at a party, he could never predict whether he would drink one beer and stop, or go on drinking until he passed out; whether he could smoke one joint and stop, or go on to use two or three other drugs and consume various kinds and quantities of alcohol. *The basic issue was not how much or how often he drank or used drugs; it was that whenever he drank or used chemicals socially, he was liable to experience a total loss of control.*

Nor is age an obstacle to chemical dependency. For nearly six years, we had told ourselves John was too young to have a serious alcohol or drug problem, yet he probably became addicted within a few months of his first exposure to pot at thirteen.

Repetitive use of a mind-altering substance, if continued long enough, will produce chemical dependency in a person of *any* age.

Disturbing recent evidence indicates that adolescents may become addicted far more quickly than adults, probably because of their undeveloped ego structure and biochemical vulnerability, particularly if there is a family history of chemical dependency. The state of alcoholism or drug addiction that takes thirty years to become full-blown in an adult may occur within two or three years for a susceptible teenager, or in just *a few months*, if cocaine or "crack" is the chemical involved. If this is so, the harvest of the chemical epidemic is only beginning, for today's young people generally start to drink and use drugs socially around the age of eleven or twelve, and cocaine use is becoming more widespread with each passing year.

The genetic factor is an important element in this equation. Our lecturer asked for a show of hands by those with one or more addicted relatives. We stared around in amazement as nearly every hand went up! Here was clear proof that alcoholism and drug addiction, inherited or not, run in families. Most researchers today do believe that the disease is a genetic one.

Bob and I counted up all the relatives we could think of who had a drinking problem. In our generation, our parents' generation, and our grandparents' generation, we counted a total of twelve individuals with a past or present drinking problem. And there were several more "questionables." We obviously had a strong family history of alcoholism, and John was the unfortunate one of our children who drew the genetic wild card.

My grandfather used to say, "I never touch liquor because I like it too well." My great-grandfather drank and was of such a cantankerous disposition that his wife issued a stock warning to visiting relatives: "Shhh! Don't rile Ned!"—a classic enabler. Our discovery of what was *really* wrong with all these "difficult" family personalities shed a great deal of light on unexplained problems over the generations.

Chemical dependency is not a curable disease, but it is treatable. It *can* be arrested, with proper education and understanding. Once addicted, a person can never return comfortably to social use of alcohol or other drugs. Abstinence is the only avenue to continued recovery. John had hoped he could learn to drink in moderation, but he knew now that he would never be able to drink or use other drugs without painful consequences.

We were told that most addicts who choose not to use mind-altering chemicals speak of themselves as recover*ing* instead of recover*ed*. They never become unaddicted or unalcoholic, but with the right kind of help they can and do become sober and drug-free, and live useful, happy lives. We families, too, will be recovering for the rest of our lives, growing beyond the unhealthy aura of the dysfunctional family system, a little bit at a time.

A hand went up in the back of the room.

"What about someone who drinks or uses drugs on the weekends, but holds down a job and looks after his family? Would you consider that person chemically dependent?"

"Look at the situation in terms of harmful dependence," said our speaker. "If the use of mind-altering chemicals is causing *any* continuing disruption in his personal, social, spiritual, or economic life, and the person does not stop the use of chemicals, there *is* dependency, and it is harmful."

Finally, we looked at the delusional elements of the disease. Blackouts are a feature of chemical dependency. A blackout is not the same thing as passing out. An addicted person who is having a blackout may appear to be functioning normally, yet will later have absolutely no recollection of what transpired during that period. We learned that John had found concert ticket stubs in his pocket, but didn't remember being at the concert; friends assured him he was there. So John had already experienced blackouts, an indication that his addiction was in an advanced stage.

Euphoric recall is another delusion. The chemically dependent man remembers having a wonderful time at the party; he doesn't remember how rude and obnoxious he was. The woman doesn't remember falling down drunk or throwing up in her date's car. This distortion of reality prevents the drinker or user from coming to grips with the unpleasant truth.

Repression also serves to block out painful memories. If John acted like a jackass, he'd rather not be reminded of it, so his psyche conveniently submerged the memory. If he called me a bitch, he conveniently forgot it.

But I couldn't possibly forget such events, and by confronting him with my memories, I could help him take an honest look at himself—bring all this garbage up from the psychological basement to be faced in the daylight, atoned for, and forgiven, then discarded once and for all.

Inaccurate feedback from family and friends keeps the issue cloudy. When I asked, "Boys, what's wrong with your eyes? They look funny," they laughed it off. If I had said, "Your eyes are frequently red, I find eyedrops in your pockets, you wear sunglasses even at night and keep dim lightbulbs in your room," all this might have begun to add up, particularly if other members of the family reinforced my observations.

Delusional thinking affected our emotional life and feelings in many ways. All of us had participated to some extent in John's delusions. We needed to unlearn dysfunctional behavior and start learning healthy responses.

"Chemical dependency is the trickiest disease in the world," our speaker told us. "It constantly assures its victims that there's absolutely nothing wrong with them." We applauded, for we knew we were starting to get well. It was a good feeling!

Does it sound crazy that we were happy to be told our child had a lifelong, incurable, potentially fatal disease? I can see that it might. Our happiness arose from our discovery that John was *not* a psychopath, *not* schizo-phrenic, *not* inherently vicious, and did *not* need to stay sick. He had made a choice to get well, and we were there to back him up.

We finally knew that we were *not* crazy, *not* bad parents, *not* worthless people, and *not* beyond hope and help. No wonder it felt so good!

Between lectures during Family Week, we participated in Group. John had been in group therapy throughout his hospital stay. Apart from John, we attended our own Family Group, made up of four other families and ourselves—brothers and sisters as well as parents, nice-looking people. Each family had a chemically dependent person in the program. Our counselor, Alice, was cheerful and encouraging.

"We're all here to share our experiences," she told us. "To get us started, I'll ask each family to describe the effects of chemically dependent behavior on your household. Who'd like to begin?"

"I don't mind being first," I heard myself say, and I launched into my recital of our nightmare: behavior problems, trouble with the law, drunkenness, staying out late and unaccounted for, car wrecks, school problems, rudeness, fits of rage, suicide threats, the lot. As I went down the list, a handsome and self-possessed father sitting in a corner began to weep quietly. Tears streamed down his face throughout my story, and I knew I was telling his story too.

As others in the room took their turns, we realized we were hearing the same story, over and over, like a broken record. There were the same drunk-driving arrests, court appearances, suspended and not-suspended sentences, lies, deceptions, fights, bad checks, repeatedly shattered hopes. A progressive and predictable illness indeed!

Having come from many different places, feeling isolated in our misery, we were suddenly surrounded by good friends, sensitive and humbled human beings who understood one another's pain. That simple communion was deeply healing. Those other families won our affections completely.

Brothers and sisters, as well as parents, mourned the loss of family members dead to affection and loving concern. One husky footballer told about life with his drug-addicted older brother, blurting out at the end, "I just didn't care about Chris—I just didn't care!" I heard a different, unspoken message: *I need to work very hard to distance myself from this beloved brother who has hurt me so much.*

When a kind and gentle family man asked how he could possibly live with the shame and embarrassment he had suffered on account of his alcoholic drug-dealing son, I felt his anguish too. We were bound to each other in the peculiar compassion of those who have known identical pain.

Alice taught us a new skill—to identify and speak our feelings. Sounds easy. For this particular group of people it was extraordinarily difficult.

Ordinarily, we said such things as, "I feel that you don't care what happens to yourself," or "I feel you need to get your life together."

But those are thoughts, not feelings. Real feelings come in three-word statements that describe emotions:

"I feel *sad*" (when you ignore me).

"I feel *angry*" (when you lie to me).

"I feel *happy*" (when I see you succeed).

Can you hear the difference? Any statement that begins, "I feel that . . ." is not a real "feeling" statement. The tip-off is the word *that,* spoken or implied.

Communicating in three-word statements is unbelievably hard for chemically dependent persons and their families. We had learned to suppress our feelings in order to survive and stay sane. Now we had to dig them up again, put names to them, and speak them.

We looked at family response to the illness. The chemically dependent person develops a relationship with the chemicals that affects all other relationships. The addict's life is centered on the chemicals and on him- or herself. Others in the family center their lives on the addict; they want to control that self-centered behavior, make up for it, hide it, blame themselves, or simply nurse the hurt.

The chemically dependent person has the same basic moral values as the rest of the family, unlikely as that may seem. But the compulsion to drink and use other drugs renders the person unable to live by those values. Driven by addiction, the person does things that conflict with his or her values, then feels guilty and ashamed. Instead of acknowledging that misery, the addict displaces that self-hatred by lashing out at others, usually family members or other loved ones. The scorn I thought John felt for me was actually a reflection of his own self-disgust.

We learned about enabling. Enablers shield the chemically dependent person from the consequences of the disease. They do not see things (I didn't see that John was stoned, and Bob saw nothing), tolerate sick behavior, assume responsibilities, protect, excuse, nag, preach, bitch. Great-grandma was a classic enabler; she made sure nobody riled Ned. I had been a first-class enabler myself, skilled in all those techniques.

Two authors have accurately depicted the roles assumed by members of an alcoholic's family, which also apply to those in families affected by other drugs: Joseph Kellermann, *Alcoholism: A Merry-Go-Round Named Denial;* Sharon Wegscheider, *Another Chance: Hope and Health for Alcoholic Families.*

These two authors also describe the *professional* enabler. Father Kellermann identifies that person as a "clergyman, doctor, lawyer or social worker" who serves to *"reduce the crisis rather than to use it to initiate a recovery program"* [italics added]. Sharon Wegscheider describes the professional enabler as "a counselor or other helping professional who engages in the same kinds of dysfunctional behavior as the family Enabler—denial, avoidance, covering up, taking responsibility for someone else, either the Dependent or another family member."

These professional enablers do not consciously sabotage recovery. They do it unknowingly. We had dealt with many unwitting professional enablers: the Treasury agent, the probation officer, both the juvenile-court and the municipal-court judge, our pastor, Dean Smith, Dr. Lannon, Dr. Luther and Elaine, Dean Allen. All these had enabled John to stay sick, believing they were helping.

Denial was the cardinal attitude that underlay all our responses. Families of chemically dependent people attribute the drinking or chemical abuse to everything under the sun: emotional problems, a divorce or death in the family, being the middle child (or the eldest, or the youngest), having a stepfather or stepmother, being too bright, having learning disabilities. You know what we said about John—that he was extremely intelligent, bored in school, high-strung, and hung around with the wrong crowd.

We couldn't see that we were dealing with a primary disease instead of a symptom. Parents who deal with a child on a daily basis fail to perceive the gradual downhill progression, while others who see the youngster less frequently find it obvious. Many people in Middletown could have told us soon after it began that John had a problem with alcohol and drugs. We couldn't see it for the life of us.

As John's disease progressed, our negative feelings had also progressed. Mike relied on a standard accusation: "You love John more than you love Susie or me! He's your little pet!" I became angry and resentful and blamed Bob for being a weak parent who wavered between harsh disciplinary measures and total permissiveness. He blamed me for standing between him and the children. Both were fair assessments of reality, but we didn't know how to manage any better. We felt trapped.

And John had his own bagful of useful projections: "You're both crazy!" "I can't be a goody-goody like you were, Mom!" "No one could live with you two. None of my friends can see how I stand living in this family." Such remarks simply fed our feelings of low self-esteem.

Our social isolation became entrenched. Dysfunctional families believe they should be able to solve their own problems; they also believe that no other family has such a problem. Every member of the family thinks he or she has somehow failed. Parents assume guilt for a child's behavior. Other children begin to exhibit emotional disturbances. Discipline in the home is inconsistent and varies with mood swings. Children feel they must take sides. Sober children become angry with the chemically dependent child for causing the family so much stress and pain. Everyone struggles to keep the Big Secret from the rest of the world, so no one will know how miserably the family has failed.

As Chief Enabler, I could feel worthy only by attempting to control John's behavior and use: limit his spending money, check up on him, leave him out of family events, make excuses for his behavior or nonappearance, dispose of any chemicals found. All such manipulation is doomed to failure. If you're trying to live with an addict, you will continue to suffer as long as you try to control the uncontrollable. Many parents of young abusers get stuck here.

"By God, if the kid lives in my house, he's not going to use drugs and drink," a parent may declare. A youngster who has merely experimented a time or two will probably stop if such an injunction is stated vigorously enough.

But a chemically dependent youngster will keep on using and drinking, no matter how stringent the strictures, until he or she receives appropriate treatment.

In Family Week I learned something I come back to again and again to keep my thinking straight. It's called The Four Cs:

> I didn't *cause* John's addiction.
> I can't *control* it.
> I can't *cure* it.
> I'm learning to *cope*.

In the end, the dysfunctional family adopts a motto: Survive and Stay Sane. Sober family members find ways to sublimate their pain: Bob's work, jogging, tennis, and gardening; my part-time job; Susan's trip to England and academic achievement; Mike's aloofness.

Wegscheider points out that older children in such a family often become overachievers (Heroes), showing the world that at least some people in the family can do something right. They find legitimate reasons to leave home, marry early, or live with someone. Younger children may be underachievers, get into trouble, seek attention, or even duplicate the career of the addict (Lost Children, Scapegoats, and Mascots). *Everyone* stuffs (suppresses) feelings and has a low sense of self-worth.

Various other responses to chemical dependency at home include becoming Peacemakers, People-pleasers, Caretakers, Black Sheep, Perfectionists, or Con Artists. Most sober family members, at one time or another, begin to think they must be crazy. And the sexual functioning of all adults is disturbed.

The strongest person in the group, the Chief Enabler, or co-dependent, takes over. The chemically dependent person's role diminishes; sober family members' roles enlarge. As Enabler, I received all the messages and responded to them; tried to keep everybody happy; found out what was going on before anybody else did; pulled the strings to make things happen.

That person needs treatment every bit as much as the addict. My body's response to my plight was already cause for concern, and I'm still working to overcome unhealthy patterns built up before and during John's illness. It takes a long time to become healthy again.

Religion often is wrongly used in the dysfunctional family setting. The chemically dependent person, who already feels ashamed, guilty, and depraved, cannot respond to the idea of a loving God. And if someone else in the family labels him or her a worthless sinner, the addict believes it's undoubtedly true, and there's no point in trying to do better.

The Chief Enabler may pray fervently and daily for God to cure the addict. Yet if the praying member fails to make the necessary hard choices that will push the person to accept help, nothing changes. When God doesn't perform the requested miracle, the praying person either retreats more determinedly into religion, or decides God has failed and abandons all claim to religious faith—more losses in the spiritual realm.

"Trust Allah," says an Arab proverb, "but tie your camel." It's a fine thing to turn things over to God, but if the disturbed family is to learn to make healthy choices again, it will need the assistance of experts who understand all the ramifications of addiction.

Until such time as the members of the family move to bring about a change, the chemically dependent member will continue to be the conscious or unconscious focus of everyone's attention. And yet the addict's effectiveness in the family system slowly dwindles away. The rest of the family usually begins to treat the person as though she or he just isn't there. After the first few years, Mike treated John this way whenever he could pull it off, and the rest of us often did the same, preferring not to talk about him or have any contact with him.

A drastic family break may come about in consequence of the miserable situation: divorce, estrangement, a runaway child, an early and calamitous marriage, or ejection of the chemically dependent person from the house. Such a break occurs when one member simply cannot stand the pressure any longer and sees no other way out.

We learned that once the adolescent becomes a habitual user, all emotional growth ceases. John was emotionally still a thirteen-year-old, though he looked like a man.

When he gave up mind-altering chemicals, his emotional development recommenced, but he would need several years to catch up to his nonaddicted peers. This knowledge was a tempering influence in the months that followed.

Whenever John's progress was disappointing, we would stop and figure back: "Let's see—by now he's moving up to fourteen (or 15, or 17)," even though chronologically, he was several years older.

We learned about the various defenses we use when we feel threatened: we deny, blame, minimize, moralize, rationalize, comply, joke, laugh, talk, intellectualize, clam up, withdraw, cry. John had used every one, and so had I.

| | |
|---|---|
| *Minimizing:* | "I just had a couple of beers!" |
| | "He was only a half-hour late." |
| *Rationalizing:* | "Everybody else does it!" |
| | "It's probably just a difficult adolescence." |
| *Denying:* | "You're crazy! I don't use drugs!" |
| | "He's too young to be an alcoholic." |
| *Complying:* | "I promise, Mom, it'll never happen again." |
| | "I'll try to treat you more like an adult, if that's what you want." |

Humor was one of John's best defenses. He could be terribly funny and often got himself out of serious trouble by clowning around. Talk was my best defense. I droned on for so long that nobody heard a thing after the third or fourth word. Bob intellectualized and withdrew. Susan cried. Mike clammed up and withdrew. Once we learned the dynamic, we spotted defense mechanisms all over the place.

We identified the get-my-way techniques: helplessness, suffering, shyness, suicide or suicide threats, worry, anger. These methods work only if the targeted person acquiesces.

We were asked to identify all the defenses and get-my-way techniques our family had used to cover up deep-seated feelings. Then we needed to get back in touch with those buried feelings, however unacceptable we thought they might be.

"How does that make you feel?" was the question we heard fifty times during Family Week. Young children know quite well what their feelings are. But in growing up, as we take on layer after layer of manners and "civilization," we lose touch with those life-giving feelings and their energy. Feelings are neither good nor bad; feelings just *are*: love, hate, fear, sadness, relief, anger, shame, concern, hope, hurt, embarrassment, joy, guilt, resentment, and all the rest.

"You shouldn't feel that way" is the remark that probably causes people the greatest emotional discomfort! We *do* feel that way! Feelings are built into the human condition. Instead of stuffing our feelings or resisting them, we must acknowledge and truly experience them.

With Alice encouraging us, we could express our feelings without putting a "good" or "bad" label on them.

Gradually we became less concerned with telling ourselves how we *ought* to feel and more adept at identifying our own feelings and those of others.

Most of us had come to the treatment center with the goal of changing another person. We desperately wanted that person to stop using chemicals. During Family Week, the truth gradually sank in that *no one* can change another person. We had to confess that we can change only ourselves. Accepting this fact is one of life's hardest tasks. But when we work at it with total honesty, and do succeed in changing ourselves, this perceived change will very likely call forth an answering change in the person we're concerned about. If I could stop preaching at John and start doing some healthy things for myself, he could stop defending himself and get on with his own recovery. The choice was his.

An extremely helpful tool for me then and afterward was a reading distributed by the hospital— "Let Go . . . " —which you will find on page 186. If you're an Enabler, read it every day until it begins to take hold.

We practiced improved communication. If I challenged, "Why don't you stop using drugs and get your life in order?" John could hear only condemnation.

Using my new skills, I could report his behavior objectively and, at the same time, assume responsibility for my own feelings: "When you stare off into the distance with your jaw set and won't talk to me, I feel rejected." That statement, he could hear as reality rather than as moral judgment.

He might respond, "I didn't know I was coming across like that. I was afraid you wouldn't listen to me. I'll try to look straight at you and say clearly what I'm thinking."

The group was truly helpful in giving feedback as we practiced these new skills. One of the fathers leveled with

# Let Go . . .

To let go does not mean to stop caring. It means I can't do it for someone else.

To let go is not to cut myself off. It's the realization that I can't control another.

To let go is not to enable, but to allow learning from natural consequences.

To let go is to admit powerlessness, which means the outcome is not in my hands.

To let go is not to try to change or blame another. It's to make the most of myself.

To let go is not to care *for,* but to care *about.*

To let go is not to fix, but to be supportive.

To let go is not to judge, but to allow another to be a human being.

To let go is not to be in the middle, arranging all the outcomes, but to allow others to effect their own destinies.

To let go is not to be protective. It's to permit another to face reality.

To let go is not to deny, but to accept.

To let go is not to nag, scold, or argue, but to search out my own shortcomings and correct them.

To let go is not to adjust everything to my desires, but to take each day as it comes and cherish myself in it.

To let go is not to criticize or regulate another, but to try to become what I dream I can be.

To let go is not to regret the past, but to grow and live for the future.

To let go is to fear less and love more.

*—Author Unknown*

me: "You come across like a bossy schoolteacher. You give long speeches, and you point your finger."

For the first time, I understood how irritating my manner could be, particularly to someone who already feels guilty and ashamed. I tried to change for the better.

Effectiveness of the feedback technique is increased tremendously when practiced by a whole group of people. If a group presents the addict with totally consistent observations, without having rehearsed it, the reality becomes impossible to deny.

A comparable undertaking is the formal *intervention* aimed at getting an addicted family member into treatment. Both Sharon Wegscheider and Vernon Johnson describe the intervention process well. If John had not agreed to enter treatment on his own, we could have set up an intervention to bring him to the necessary turning point. If one-on-one didn't work, we could have confronted him as a group with the unpleasant realities of his disease, as the only way to break through the massive smoke screen of denial and delusion. We who knew him best would be an accurate mirror of reality.

With these methods under our belts, we were ready to meet John again. The encounter took place at midweek, in John's therapy group supervised by Len, its counselor. The moment was a scary one. We had come prepared with individual lists of actions that had hurt, saddened, or embarrassed us. The prospect of confronting John with such unwelcome information was scary. We had been told to state times, places, and circumstances as specifically as we could, and report factually what had happened and how we had felt about the event then and later.

When we joined John's group, we found ourselves in a circle that included ten other young people much like him. There were some bizarre haircuts, a lot of ragged jeans, and what felt like hostile stares all around. All these young addicts had fought their own battles with family members, and we represented the species.

Len spelled out the rules. The first day, Bob, Mike, and I would speak. John would listen without responding. The group would give feedback, followed by discussion of issues that came up. The next day, John would tell us his side of things, and once again the group's feedback would keep us in touch with all sides of reality.

As our encounter progressed, this circle of sensitive young men and women generously opened up to let us in. They observed fairly what we said and how we said it, called our hand when we were out of line, called John's when he read us wrong or was less than honest, and gave us plenty of affirmation when we seemed to be right.

At the outset, John stared fixedly at me, a gaze that came across as hostility and defiance. He began to move about restlessly soon after I launched upon my list:

1. Discovery at the beach of the marijuana and John's violent response to my getting rid of it.
2. The day he and Mike went hunting and came in stoned.
3. The many nights I didn't know where he was and had to call people to track him down.
4. All the times he came in with red eyes and slurred speech, walked unsteadily, and verbally abused me.
5. The afternoon he carried his gun into the woods and fired until he was out of ammunition.
6. His anger when I questioned him about finances.
7. His two arrests, the hearing, and the trial.

8. His recent physical complaints of chest pain, cough, sniffles, no energy or stamina.
9. Parents' Weekend at Chambers, his rejection of Bob and me.
10. Being blackballed during Rush.
11. The Christmas Eve he, Mike, and Lanny got high in the garage.
12. The Colorado fiasco and our anxiety and anger.
13. His going to Syracuse over our objections, his crazy talk about the Grateful Dead, our fears for his sanity and survival.
14. Our concern about the amount he was drinking that last summer, the pothead friends he hung around with.
15. My sadness each year at Christmas and on his birthday, when I couldn't think of a single thing to give him, because I knew him so little.

When Bob's turn came, he alluded to an additional fifteen circumstances that I had either forgotten or never been told about. Mike's list was briefer but still entirely different. If Susan had been there, her list would very likely have been unique too. It dawned on us that had we pooled our information years before and put the parts of the puzzle together, we would have solved our mystery much sooner. Taken as a whole, John's behavior painted an overwhelmingly pathologic picture. We thought we were protecting him, but we all actually were enablers, standing in the way of his recovery.

John appeared acutely uncomfortable as we itemized these unhappy events. He wanted to dispute what we were saying and justify himself, but Len reminded him to hold his comments for the next day.

By this time, the other group members were listening

with great interest. Until now, John apparently had been reporting highly selective versions of these happenings. Many events we brought up had never been mentioned to the group at all.

More than once a group member spoke up: "Well, John! You didn't tell us about *that*, man."

By the end of our recital, John's head was bowed, his face buried in his hands. I felt immensely sorry for him, but there was no other way. The pain on both sides had to be exposed before it could be healed.

During Bob's turn, he had mentioned a vial of white powder found in the back seat of John's car. "What was in that tube, John?"

John looked questioningly at Len.

Len nodded. "You can answer to give information."

"It was supposed to be cocaine, but I didn't get a chance to try any before you got rid of it."

Mike, who knew the truth, spoke up. "Not even a little bit, John?"

John hesitated. "Well, yeah, some."

He couldn't stonewall any longer, for Mike had the goods on him. The group was quick to jump on John's evasion.

This was a sickening moment for me. I faced the fact that he was still living in the old patterns—lying, sliding, slipping by. Mike, on the other hand, was changing. His healthy truthful impulse had carried him through before the old loyalties could hold him back.

This was a big breakthrough. John was forced to face up to his habitual lying and the fact that he was still trying to get away with it.

On the other hand, I abandoned my fantasy that everything would be perfect once he stopped doing drugs. John was still going to be John. Even if he chose to live a drug-free life hereafter, we would still relate to each other in unhealthy ways from time to time.

At the end of the session John looked about ready to explode. "Len, I need to say something."

"Okay. Keep it short."

"I'm feeling really frustrated here. I feel that Mike, Mom, and a couple of others here are pointing fingers at me. When I first came in this hospital, I stopped feeling so guilty, because someone finally told me, 'You have a disease that makes you like this.' But now I'm feeling guilty again, like you're all telling me, 'You worthless piece of trash, you scum.' "

"You're a day ahead," said Len. "Save it for tomorrow."

The lecture that night was illustrated by thoroughly graphic slides: diseased liver tissue, hemorrhagic blood vessels, cross-sections of brain tissue destroyed by years of chronic intoxication. Nauseated, I turned my head away.

John was watching me from the other side of the room. Even though we were not supposed to communicate until Group the next day, he crossed the room quietly, slipped into the chair next to mine, and slid an arm around me.

That night I wrote in my journal, "Love is what does the healing here. Love *can* cure the pain, if it's coupled with courage and truth. If I care enough about John to keep on loving him and trying to reach him with the truth, perhaps he will care enough to love himself and get well. I can only hope."

Love, courage, and truth—we finally were in possession of the keys to freedom.

# CHAPTER ELEVEN

# Taking It All Back Home

_____ *B*ob and I talked about what was happening to us. Having expected the hospital stay to be depressing, he was surprised by a sense of lightness and exhilaration. He felt deeply connected with the treatment process, knowing the lecturers and counselors were absolutely on target in everything they were teaching us.

"It's been like a conversion experience," he said wonderingly, "an intense joy, stemming from the knowledge that we're getting to the bottom of our troubles at last. I know we're finally in the right place."

My feelings were much the same. The emotional intensity of our group sessions stirred me deeply, after so many years of suppressing highly charged feelings. Each time the group met, we were moved by a powerful force compounded of pain, courage, honesty, and tenderness.

All the families were compiling lists of their painful experiences, presenting them in Group to their chemically dependent members, and accepting the response with humility. The group members dealt faithfully with the material and the way it was presented, giving feedback, hauling us over, around, and through our defenses to a place where healing could begin.

The work was fraught with risk and vulnerability, but when we took that risk and reached out to one another in our hurting, we came out feeling affirmed, clean, and true. Our hearts were being purified of all the old anger, hatred, and sickness. None of us could have done this work alone. We needed one another to accomplish it.

Almost every night during Family Week, I dreamed—vivid, powerful, moving dreams. One dream in particular stood out. I was having enormous difficulty accepting the fact that I simply could not change John—that he and only he could make the choices that would lead him to health and recovery. In my pride, I clung desperately to the belief that it was still all up to me, Supermom. And when my intellectual and emotional powers failed to get me to the essential place of surrender, this stunning dream did the work.

It was a dream of seduction, involving John and me, a dream in which I was caught between an overwhelming physical attraction for my son and the equally over-whelming knowledge that such a connection between us was unthinkable. For one desperate moment in that dream, I was willing to risk any consequences, no matter how terrible, in order to experience that ecstatic sensual connection.

The impact of this dream was incalculable. I saw at once that our relationship had to change, that I must be "seducing" John to remain dependent upon me by subconsciously allowing, even encouraging him to behave in sick ways. Clearly, I had no choice but to back off entirely, so that he could grow up well and whole.

That powerful and stirring dream accomplished in a few minutes something that would have required days in any other circumstances. Through it, I touched upon a spiritual level deeper than anything I had known before.

Although the material of my dream was powerfully disturbing, its message was sacred on the most profound level—the level that would lead both John and me to wholeness.

Bob also had a powerful dream during Family Week. The group perceived early on that Bob's interactions with John always shifted from painful emotion to sterile intellectuality. Whenever an encounter became intense, Bob would convert the whole thing to a mind game, and suddenly both he and John became calm, superrational, and invulnerable. It was a though a couple of wildcats had suddenly sat down to a meditative game of chess.

John played right along with this defense. He was quite bright enough to relate to Bob intellectually, and doing so got *him* off the emotional hot seat. The group told Bob he needed to break out of this intellectualizing, but he couldn't grasp what was called for.

And so a dream did the work for him as well. He dreamed he was in an operating room, gowned, masked, and gloved, with assistants at his side. Beneath the brilliant overhead lights, he held a chainsaw poised above the head of the motionless, anesthetized patient. Bob's task was to saw directly through the patient's head— skull, brain and all—and continue through the neck and body to the living, beating heart. With fear and trembling, he did cut through, straight to the heart. It continued to beat, and the patient lived and was cured.

Whenever he and John were tempted to slip into their mind games thereafter, Bob remembered that throbbing heart and stayed with his emotions, however disturbing, until the necessary transactions were accomplished.

Mike kept his reactions to Family Week to himself. He had his own room at the motel, and we left him to do as he pleased after dinner while we attended the evening lectures. He didn't talk much about the happenings of the day, although Family Week was undoubtedly an intense experience for him. He participated willingly in Group, but he was not ready to share his feelings. We respected his need for privacy and relief, confident that he would work it all out in his own way and time.

Finally John's turn came to speak in Group. He sat forward on the edge of his seat and faced us fiercely.

"Okay, John," said Len. "Today you have the floor."

John took a deep breath. "Right. Okay. Mom, Dad, I want to say first that you have never accepted my friends." His voice shook. "You say they're rude, they don't talk to you, you don't like their looks. I resent that, because they're my friends."

I wanted to say they were all as sick as John, but the rules forbade me to speak. Bob watched intently as John forged ahead. Mike sat with his chair tipped back against the wall, arms folded, waiting to see what would happen next.

John swallowed hard and continued. "You don't like my ways of spending my time, going to Grateful Dead concerts, listening to my tapes, going out with my friends. That makes me angry."

The eyes of the other group members were darting from one to another of us, assessing our reactions, waiting to see where feedback was needed.

John's breathing was shallow and rapid, and his list quivered in his hands. His task was daunting, but he went ahead courageously.

"You don't like my hair, my clothes, you don't like anything about me. Nothing I do pleases you. I feel hurt and angry about that."

I wanted to cry out that I loved him, this child I had borne and cared for so lovingly. I knew I must not. We waited, silent.

"And ever since I can remember, you've always held Susan up like some kind of a goddess!" His voice rose, his emotion building. "*Susan* can do no wrong! *Susan's* perfect! You're always telling everybody how wonderful she is, but all you do is criticize me! And I feel really hurt and resentful!"

It was our turn to listen, not just with our ears, but with our hearts.

And now the tears rose in John's eyes and spilled down his cheeks.

"Just *once* in my life," he blurted out, "I wish you would appreciate me the way you appreciate Susie! Just *once*! You don't know much much it hurts to hear you go on and on about how *smart* she is, how *cute,* how much you love her and Dave, all the things you love about them! I think you don't love *anything* about me!"

An intense silence filled the room when John was done. Could he not know that we were all sitting here at Christmastime, a thousand miles from home, on hard chairs in a drab little room with ice on the windows, simply because we loved and appreciated him? No, he could not. He was too deeply embedded in a state of rock-bottom self-esteem, compounded by an inability to let anyone know his feelings or to perceive the true feelings of others.

No matter how we complimented or praised John, it came across to him as condemnation because of the way he felt about himself. He had forgotten our praise for his banjo playing and his National Merit recognition, our laughter at his jokes, Susan's eagerness to have him at Chambers, our longing to share his life in spite of his defiant refusal to let us in. John's guilt and hurt were so deep that he could survive only by projecting his self-loathing onto others. He could not imagine we could love him just as he was.

Len invited the group to respond. Several members complimented John on the courageous way he had stated his feelings.

"That had to be hard, man."

"Yeah, you said what you had to say to your mom and dad, and you let your feelings show."

"Can I respond to some of John's statements?" I asked.

"Group?"

"Okay."

"Yeah."

"Let's hear it."

"John, I wish you could know what's in my heart. The whole time you were talking, I wanted desperately to tell you how much I care about you. We couldn't like your friends, your pastimes, because your whole life was drug-centered and your friends were all druggies.

"Susan is not one bit more important to this family than you are. It's just that she hasn't caused us as much pain as you have.

"When I look at you, I see a beautiful, fine, loving person locked up inside, and I'm not giving up until that person comes out." Now my tears were flowing too. "I'm here, son, because I love you with all my heart, and I'll move heaven and earth to get you to where you need to be, so you can become the person I know you really are."

The group heard that without comment.

Len responded. "Betsy, did you read the page in your folder called 'Let Go'?"

"Yes."

"I think you'd better read it again. John's recovery is not up to you."

I balked. "If he could do it by himself, I wouldn't be here."

"You're here chiefly for *yourself,* not for John. You said you would move heaven and earth to get him to where he needs to be. You can't do it. Only *John* can do it, with the help of his Higher Power."

Suddenly I felt very humble. "I hear you."

John held up his hand. "I'd like to say something."

"Go ahead."

"I'm still having a hard time with feeling guilty and ashamed. I think you're putting that guilt trip on me, Mom. You're saying how much you're willing to do to help me be who I need to be, but telling me I'm a piece of trash and a scumbag isn't what I need to hear."

"Whoa, John!" Tina said from the other side of the circle. "*I* didn't hear anybody say 'a piece of trash or a scumbag.' "

"My mom did."

"Hey, man! Nobody said it," argued Tim, another group member. "You might have heard it, but nobody said it."

John looked to Len for confirmation. "She didn't say I was a piece of trash or a scumbag?"

"No, John, she didn't. She said she believed you were a fine person, and she wanted to help that fine person come out."

Astonishingly, John had heard words nobody had said, conjuring them up out of thin air and his own negative self-image.

Ralph, a father, raised his hand. "I have some feedback for Betsy."

"Okay, Ralph."

"Betsy, while you're saying to John, 'You're great,' it

sounds to me like 'You're great, John, *but*—' There's always an unspoken qualifier. I hear you telling him, 'You're great if you do what *I* think you should.' "

"Good feedback, Ralph."

"Yeah, I heard it too," said Tim.

"Thanks. I can accept that." The group helped me see that I could seem threatening, come across as rigid and judgmental. At the same time, they were sending me another message: *You're a person of worth and value, and we care about you enough to give you an honest picture of yourself.*

As Family Week went on, we all gained new insights. Bob learned he had been suppressing feelings for years. He had never said "I love you" to his own parents, although he did love them deeply. His interactions with our three children were either assignment of tasks, sports played on his own terms (perfection), or intellectual exercises of some sort. He learned to listen lovingly as others expressed their feelings, to share activities in an attitude of mutuality, and to short-circuit his intellect in favor of his heart.

Mike learned to be honest about his own partying, something he'd done out of a desire to fit in with others and, perhaps, to emulate John. He learned compassion for his brother as he gained an understanding of John's illness. Most important, he learned to deal with feelings. Mike was speaking once in Group when Alice interrupted him.

"Excuse me, Mike, there's something I've been wanting to say to you. This has been happening all week in Group, and I think it's time to tell you about it. Whenever anyone else gets close to the point of tears or actually starts to cry, I notice you jump into the conversation and distract us from whatever it is that's making the person sad. You remind me of the southern belle who never lets the conversation linger on unpleasant subjects.

"And if it's you who feels like crying, you stuff the feeling and clam up until it goes away. I perceive you as being very uncomfortable with tears. How do you feel about that?"

"I just think it's a waste of time when people cry. We should get onto something more productive," said Mike.

"You're telling me what you *think*, Mike, not what you feel. But I hear you," said Alice. "Remember that those tears and feelings are very important to the person who's crying. Whatever is making someone sad is the kind of thing we're here to talk about. Otherwise, we can never work through it.

"Next time anyone cries or is about to cry, just keep quiet and let them do it, okay? And if you feel like crying yourself, go ahead and let the tears come."

"Okay," Mike replied with a diffident shrug. Thereafter, when others cried, he kept still. But Mike himself never shed a tear.

Before we were through, we had dumped a ton of poisonous emotional garbage in that little room. We began to relearn to trust one another, to care for one another, and to really love one another. I can never forget the grace and power at work among those young addicts. They gave us the paramount gift of unflinching honesty and unconditional acceptance. They gave us back our life as a family.

A final celebration took place the night before we were to leave for home. John had a pass to leave the hospital with us for six hours. We caught a taxi to a shopping center by the river, a delightful spot centered on a small ice-skating rink, with many inviting restaurants and shops. It was fun just to wander through the place, to see John at ease and reestablishing contact with the everyday world.

Later we went out to dinner. All four of us were a little nervous, for this was a sort of rehearsal for what it would be like to take the "new" John home with us. I wondered whether this meal would be like all the ones in the past when we had to handle John with kid gloves, whether there would be ugly remarks and hurt feelings. And of course, there was the overriding question of how John would deal with alcohol.

John himself made the generous gesture that put us all at ease. Holding up his glass of water, he saluted us: "I'd like to propose a toast."

Eager to please, we lifted our water glasses too.

"Here's to my newfound sobriety," John said with a pleased grin.


At the hospital, some final details had to be dealt with. Bob, Mike, and I met with Len to discuss our concerns about John: his ability to con people and whether that behavior would stop; the return to Chambers and the chemically oriented social life of college; his Deadhead attachments. Len had a good grasp of what made John tick. We were all appropriately cautious about his ability to continue his recovery. He was not cured, but he had given every indication of a sincere beginning. Len was confident that the strong family system would give him a great deal of the support he was going to need.

We all met with Charlene, John's counselor. She gave him a written aftercare plan. He was to attend three A.A. or N.A. meetings each week, read his recovery literature faithfully, get a sponsor in either A.A. or N.A., and stay in touch with Charlene by telephone.

After three months, he could return to the hospital for a follow-up visit, another at six months, a third at one year, and a final one at two years. After that, he would be considered discharged.

Bob and I asked Charlene how we should monitor John's adherence to this program.

"He knows what he has to do to keep his recovery working," she told us. "It's his responsibility and his choice. The best thing you can do is let him know you're behind him with loving support and encouragement. But *don't* try to work his program for him."

"We'll try to remember. And thank you."

"Thanks, Charlene." John stood up to leave. "I have to see my spiritual counselor in a few minutes. I need to do my Fifth Step before I go home."

"Good. Take care of yourself, John, and keep in touch. Just take it *one day at a time,* and *keep it simple.*"

John smiled as he picked up on the familiar A.A. slogans.

While John met with his spiritual counselor, the rest of us returned to Family Group—our last day within this circle of loving friends. We all shared our anxiety about having our chemically dependent family members back at home, facing honestly the likelihood that not everything would go smoothly.

"Your family members have accomplished just 20 percent of their recovery here in the hospital," said Alice. "The other 80 percent will take place after they're back with you."

We had already seen a tremendous change in John. If

this change represented only a small part of his total recovery, we could expect great things ahead.

"Don't expect too much too soon," Alice cautioned. "It took your chemically dependent folks a long time to get as sick as they were when they came here. It will take them a long time to become solidly healthy again."

Mike threw out a cogent question: "What should I do if I feel like having a beer around John? Should I have it in front of him? Should I offer him one? Or should I try not to let him know I'm drinking?"

"I'm glad you brought that up, Mike. I've been waiting for an opportunity to open something up with both you and Fred." Fred was the same age as Mike and also had an older brother in treatment.

"I'd like for you two fellows to go the Intake Unit before you leave for home, and ask to be evaluated for chemical dependency. There's enough question in my mind about your own drinking and using patterns that I think you should get an expert opinion before you leave."

"I'll be glad to," said Mike. "I'd like to find out for myself. I've been wondering about some things while I've been here."

Fred, a suave young man who looked older than his seventeen years, shrugged carelessly.

"Fine with me. I don't think I have a problem, but I'm willing to check it out, if you think it's important."

"I suggest the two of you go on down there now. We'll finish up here and see you at lunch."

Bob and I exchanged puzzled glances, as did Fred's parents. Were we dealing with two addicts?

"No time like the present to find out," said Bob resignedly. "If that's the way it is, we'll deal with it."

Mike came to lunch late, wearing a relieved expression.

"What did they tell you, son?"

"They say I'm an abuser, but not an addict. I'm not chemically dependent, but they say there are enough worrisome signs that I should try six months of abstinence and see what happens. If I can't do it, I'll probably need to come back for treatment. If I can do it, I don't have a problem—at least not right now."

I could see that Mike took this admonition seriously and intended to live by it. Life at home would certainly be different, with two sober, drug-free young men in the house! Bob and I had already agreed to have no alcohol around while John was living with us. Abstaining and declining to serve alcohol to our friends was a small sacrifice when we considered that John would have to abstain every single day for the rest of his life.

We attended John's Group for the last time. He was there, back from his Fifth Step conference. In that step, the chemically dependent person admits to God, to himself, and to another human being the nature of his wrongs. John's face and the faces of the other group members who had just completed their Fifth Step told us what a powerful experience it had been. Young men and women who had appeared lifeless and pale the day before now joined us bright-eyed, rosy-cheeked, and very much alive. Confession *is* good for the soul. The faces of those young people carried their newfound health and wholeness like a banner in the breeze.

Our family stood by, deeply touched, as Len presented John's medallion—a token of work done, a symbol of growth and transformation. John stood proudly to receive it. Then group members came forward one by one to give him rib-crushing hugs, to tell him they loved him, to wish him well. John then presented Bob, Mike, and me with our own medallions, made a little speech and hugged us.

Today, wherever I am, my medallion is there with me. On one side is a butterfly, symbolizing new life, and on the other side, a version of Reinhold Niebuhr's Serenity Prayer beloved by recovering people everywhere:

God grant me the serenity
To accept the things I cannot change,
Courage to change the things I can,
And wisdom to know the difference.

We arrived home in time for the Christmas Eve midnight service. At the last minute, John said he'd rather not go. We had learned that religious life is the earliest loss in addiction and the last gain in recovery. The lecturer had told us not to make an issue of religious observances but to allow the recovering family member to make such decisions.

I kissed John on the cheek. "We'll miss you, but you do whatever makes you most comfortable."

"Thanks, Mom." He returned my kiss and looked grateful. "Oh, and by the way, Merry Christmas!"

John may not have been sitting in our pew that night, but that was just a technicality. We were a family reunited. I thought of the earlier December when we had called on Lanny's parents to tell them about the dope-smoking episode. This Christmas Eve was an ending and a beginning. We had come so far!

From time to time, I still hark back to the unhappy events of the past. We will never lose that past entirely. I look back on it now as a necessary evil, part of a creative process that has brought us to where we are today.

John was born with the genetic inability to handle any and all mind-altering drugs. There was no way in twentieth-century America that he could escape falling victim. His particular combination of physiological vulnerability, family maladjustment, poor coping skills, and a drug-saturated social environment made addiction inevitable. If we could have changed any one of these factors, the outcome might have been different.

But the past was only a prelude. That first Christmas Eve in recovery, our family was stronger, more loving, more honest, more confident, and less fearful, because of John's illness. And he is a greater person, with a larger capacity for honesty and love because of his illness and recovery.

Our holiday celebration was unique for us. Before we got home, we had telephoned friends who had a key to our house and asked them to pick up our modest stock of liquor and wine. It was the first time we had ever observed Christmas or New Year's without a drink in the house, and it was the most delightful holiday ever. We adopted a new drink we call a Minnesota Cocktail—apple juice and seltzer. It's delicious!

Susan and Dave arrived in time to open the Christmas gifts. As we sat around afterward amid the crumpled wrapping paper and ribbons, she spoke through happy tears.

"This has been the very best Christmas of my life."

Although she hadn't participated in Family Week, she understood that John had been brought back from a living death. The pain she had suffered on account of his addiction, rather than killing her love from her brother, had merely driven it underground. Now Susan was rediscovering how much she cared for him, how much she admired his candor and courage, how much fun it was just to be with him.

And John, having let go of his resentment of Susan, allowed himself the joy of telling her he loved her. They wrestled on the floor like a couple of eight-year-olds, watched "Star Trek" and "Gilligan's Island," talked Pig Latin—all the goofy things he had missed during his alienated adolescence.

Dave accepted all this in good fun. He remembered how much pain she had endured on John's account. He told John how happy he was for his recovery, how proud he was that he had taken the brave steps he needed to take.

Mike just reveled in the lightened atmosphere of our household. He no longer needed to escape or protect himself. He gave himself over to being the little brother again and piled gleefully on Susie and John as they rolled around on the floor. They were having fun, and they deserved it.

# CHAPTER TWELVE

# The Pieces Fall into Place

After the holidays we settled down to real life. Susan and Dave went home and back to work. Mike returned to high school. Bob went back to his practice. I had my editing and writing. Only John was left at loose ends, with two months to wait before he could return to Chambers for spring quarter.

We still had grave concerns about John's ability to restructure his life. His only friends were his old drug-using buddies and the Deadhead crowd. All these associations had to change if he was to maintain his recovery; sober friends are essential to a sober life.

Then there was Amy. She'd been a casual drinker and drug-user, but she was not addicted. John was eager to see her after their long separation. Amy had never known John sober and drug-free. This newly composed, candid, and caring young man would be like a stranger to her, someone to get to know all over again. Would she accept him? We had to wait and see.

Fortunately, John was happy to attend support-group meetings in the early days of his recovery. Middletown had no active Narcotics Anonymous chapter at that time, but there was plenty of A.A. support. John attended A.A.

several times a week and found it most helpful. The loving acceptance of that group in those first days was a basic foundation stone in his recovery.

Mike often went to A.A. meetings with John, trying to get off on the right foot with his own program. He never stood up to say, "I'm Mike and I'm an alcoholic," but he listened and learned a great deal. For the first time, he really understood that abstaining from alcohol and drugs is a choice between life and death for many. His compassion for John and other chemically dependent persons continued to grow.

Bob and I were lucky to discover a parent support group of our own. Based on the Twelve Steps of A.A., this group gave us an all-important community of understanding friends. We had only five members at the outset, but those five were faithful and committed. Since then our fellowship has continued to grow and has provided strength and encouragement to many. A score of substance-abusing youngsters in our community have found their way to help as their families have learned to recognize and deal effectively with the disease of chemical dependency.

The first serious test of John's sobriety, and of our ability to let go, was not long in coming. John announced that he was planning to meet Amy and some Deadhead friends for an all-night radio broadcast of the Grateful Dead. This was the thing we'd dreaded most—reentry into the Deadhead world. During Family Week the counselors advised us to discuss our anxiety openly with John and ask him to surround himself with several sober, drug-free people as a safeguard against temptation. Here was a chance to practice our new communication skills.

"John, I get scared when I know you'll be with your using friends again," I told him.

Bob joined in. "I'm worried you won't be able to resist the temptation to use, and I'm afraid you'll get caught in a drug bust."

"I understand your concerns," said John. "I'll try to deal with them as best I can."

We set out some conditions. We asked John to have at least two sober, drug-free companions and promise to leave his friends and find other accommodations if the pressure to use was too great. If all else failed, he was to call the local A.A. hotline.

John agreed to our requests. Amy would be there, and she had already told John she was giving up drugs and alcohol to support him in his recovery. A second sober person would be along—Tom Warren, a friend of John's from the freshman year at Chambers. Tom had left school to go through treatment even before John and was maintaining a good recovery.

"Going through treatment sure helped Tom," John told us. "Last time I saw him at a Dead show, the only thing he had was two six-packs of root beer! I think he and Amy will be all the support I need."

In spite of John's compliance, we couldn't put much faith in his promises. We had been burned too many times. Broken promises, clever deceptions, and outright lies were hard to forget. We were struggling hard to live into our own recovery.

"If life's going to be different," Bob said, "we have to start learning to trust again. Remember that slogan we learned in Family Week? *Let go and let God.*"

It was a very practical help. I repeated those five words inwardly many times after John drove off. I must have said "Let go!" to myself twenty times an hour—every time the old panicky feelings struggled to take over. And we slept easily that night, trusting John to handle the situation.

At noon the next day he was back home with a big grin of satisfaction. Amy was with him. They'd gotten up early and eaten a big breakfast with Tom before heading home in the sunny stillness of the winter morning. The three of them were the only ones without hangovers in the group of a dozen. Feeling great, they wanted to get out into the world and shout with the sheer joy of being alive and well. We honored the victory with exuberant hugs all around.

Amy stayed for a few days, renewing her ties to John as he told her of his experiences in treatment. She attended a support group meeting with Bob and me and found it helpful for her relationship with the "new" drug-free John. We saw that Amy cared deeply for him. Bubbling over with happiness for his recovery, she confessed she had worried terribly about him.

"I always knew John was a super person," she said. "But he was killing himself with drugs, and I was killing myself trying to get him to stop! Now I understand why he couldn't stop—at least not until he got the help he needed."

Amy left for Chambers, and John's plans for returning were shaping up well. We'd been wondering about a roommate, knowing he would need the close support of at least one sober, drug-free friend. Tom Warren had reappeared at just the right time. He would be returning to Chambers and needed a sober roommate too, so they happily agreed to team up. Everything to support and enhance John's recovery was being provided.

In the meantime he needed a job. He went back to the country club and asked the manager if he could fill in tending bar again. Sometimes I believe John enjoys putting himself in the riskiest possible situations. Tending bar surely can't be a desirable job for a newly sober alcoholic. But John insisted he could handle it, and we left the choice up to him.

He got the job with no difficulty, and it was good to have him out of the house every day on a definite schedule. I could get down to my own work again.

At the country club, the locker-room crowd didn't know about his hospitalization, nor did his boss or his fellow workers. They just assumed he had dropped out of college, and the barflies and card players made him the butt of their wisecracks.

"You push that bar rag around a few more years, boy, you'll be wishing you'd stayed in school!"

John took it all in silence, containing his resentment until he got home.

"You know what, Mom? I wanted to tell about twenty people today, 'Well, at least I *did* something about *my* alcohol problem, and here you are, just an old country-club drunk,' but I didn't say it. *Detach, detach,* I kept telling myself. *Live and let live.*"

His A.A. program was really helping him meet life's challenges.

One morning shortly before he returned to Chambers, John came down to breakfast looking worried. He sat down at the table, staring abstractedly into the distance.

"Anything wrong, son?" Bob asked.

"A dream I had. It was really scary, and I don't know what it means."

"Well, eat a little breakfast," I said, "then tell us about it. My grandmother always said it was bad luck to tell your dreams before breakfast."

John laughed, sipped his coffee cautiously, and started on his cereal. But halfway through, he put down his spoon.

"I *have* to tell you," he said. "If I don't share this with somebody, I think I may explode."

We gave him our full attention.

"Okay. In this dream I was somewhere standing on the seashore. I don't know exactly where it was, but it seemed familiar. I stood there on this flat, sandy beach and watched the waves as they rolled in, one after another. I felt almost hypnotized as I stood there looking out to sea.

"Soon I became aware of something strange on the horizon. At first I couldn't tell what it was. This thing gradually got closer, the waves bringing it in to shore. After a while, I realized it was an enormous pumpkin, riding the waves like a ship. I was amazed. I called it the Pumpkin Galleon. I couldn't take my eyes off it.

"As I watched, it kept bobbing on the water, coming closer and closer, until finally one gigantic breaker tossed it right up to where I stood. It struck the shore with tremendous force and burst into pieces.

"I was horrified when I saw what was inside." His face mirrored his fear. "It was full of bodies, dead bodies! They were piled up in heaps, horrible, rotten and decaying.

"I felt sick. I was so afraid, the only thing I could think of was getting away. And that was the end of the dream. When I woke up, my heart was beating like crazy, and I was covered with sweat. What do you think it can mean?"

We thought about it in silence for a bit.

"If you felt such strong emotions, the dream must have deep personal meanings for you," I said. "Can you go into it a little bit? Start off with the image of a pumpkin. What do you associate with a pumpkin?"

"Halloween," John said promptly.

"Okay. What happened at Halloween?"

"I went to a Deadhead party."

"Yes? And what happened there?"

John's expression suddenly changed to one of awe. He had made a significant connection. In a subdued voice he said, "That was the last time I tripped on acid."

"All right. And who was inside the Pumpkin Galleon?"

"Dead people. The Dead."

"Can you do the rest of it?"

"I think I can. The wreck of the Pumpkin Galleon is what would have happened to me if I'd stayed with the Deadheads and kept on doing what I was doing on Halloween. In one way it was neat and fantastic, like a fairy story, but the people inside the pumpkin had lost control of their destiny. They were dead. Yes, I see. It makes sense."

About this same time, Mary, a friend in our support group, had a crisis with her addicted son Trey. She and her family were able to persuade Trey to go to treatment and chose the same hospital in Minnesota where John's recovery had begun. Trey was there when John made his three-month follow-up visit before he returned to school. The two young men became acquainted and made plans for the coming summer, when they would both be back home, to go to A.A. meetings together.

Getting back into the mainstream of college life was a tonic for John. He called and wrote frequently to let us know how happy he was. Welcomed back enthusiastically by their friends, John reported that he and Tom had already been to an A.A. meeting and planned to attend regularly.

With his head clear, John found schoolwork a breeze. He took great pride in the papers he sent home for us to see. In spite of his past excesses, his keen intellect was all there and in high gear. When grades came out, he called to tell us he'd made the Dean's List, but was disappointed he hadn't made straight As!

I couldn't resist. "Wait a minute, John. What about that fellow who had no intention of making anything higher than a C? I guess he must not be around any more."

John laughed heartily. "You're right. He's not here."

Soon afterward, we had a note from John's compassionate professor Dr. Callahan:

Dr. and Mrs. White,
What a delight it has been to see John again. He has a sparkle in his eye, a light I hadn't seen before; he looks slim and fit and is standing up tall. His whole presence is a confident and self-assured one. John's a good man; I see much potential in him. He told me that his time in Minnesota was the best thing that could have happened to him, and that there is nobody in the world he would rather spend time with than you two.

With continuing best wishes,

The next big hurdle was Commencement. John wanted to stay to see some of his friends graduate. There would be booze and drugs, but only John could choose how to handle it. He stayed for a few parties, then came home ahead of schedule.

"When you get right down to it," he said, "being the only sober guy at the party is pretty boring." His comment was more meaningful than we knew.

When John came home for the summer, we were beginning to think his problems were over, but our "honeymoon" was short-lived. The awakening came when we learned that he had attended only that first A.A. meeting after returning to school. Our-Son-the-Con-Man found his old habits of deception terribly difficult to break. He had led us to believe he was continuing to attend the meetings by dropping suggestions and leaving the rest to our hopeful imaginations.

And we also discovered he had his first "slip" during the Commencement festivities. He had talked himself into it this way: "Everybody's leaving in a couple of days. What difference will it make if I have just a little crumb of these 'shrooms? They're a natural substance, anyway. And maybe they were wrong at the hospital. Maybe I'm *not* really chemically dependent."

So he took the hallucinogen, but he didn't enjoy it. The experience reinforced everything he'd been told about his disease. He *was* alcoholic and addicted. He could not handle alcohol or other drugs, then or ever.

When the truth came out, we were disappointed, but it didn't hurt nearly as much as we had imagined. John realized he'd gotten cocky and was not as emotionally healthy as he'd been telling himself.

Bob and I had not taken seriously the long-term implications of chemical dependency. The most positive thing we could say was that we reacted without resentment or anger. We didn't feel personally affronted that John had misled us, but viewed his deception and using as symptoms of a lingering illness. We were no more angry than we would have been if a diabetic child had had an insulin reaction. It was a healthy change in our thinking.

As we puzzled about how and why John's slip had occurred, I came across an excellent resource, Jack Mumey's *Sitting in the Bay Window: A Book for Parents of Young Alcoholics* (retitled *Young Alcoholics* in a later edition). The greatest fear of anyone close to a recovering person is that he or she will have a slip or a relapse—a full-blown return to drinking or using. Ignoring that fear will not make it go away. Chemical dependency is not curable; it can only be arrested. The potential for relapse will always be there. Mumey's discussion of the appropriate handling of an impending relapse was a great help.

We had to look at the situation honestly. We talked about the slip with John, why it had happened and what we could learn from it. It actually gave us an opportunity to better understand the disease and its consequences for the long haul. All of us were alerted to warning signs of a B.U.D.—Mumey's term for Building Up to Drink. We thought we'd see it coming next time and nip the B.U.D. in the bud.

In light of these discoveries, Bob and I felt obliged to lay down some conditions for John's living at home, even if only for the summer. We told him he was welcome as long as he did the things necessary for his recovery—attend A.A. regularly, work his program, accept fair feedback, and strive to be open and honest. Out of our own need for a predictable, orderly life, we asked him to be home by midnight or call and let us know why he couldn't make it.

John accepted these conditions. He went back to A.A. and latched onto the recovery program with renewed commitment. He appreciated the wisdom and support he found among the old-timers—those with twenty or thirty years' worth of sobriety. After that, we never had to remind him about meetings. He always went cheerfully and of his own accord.

John ran into Trey again at A.A. Once again a need was met. In Trey, John had another sober, straight friend of his own age. Together they went to A.A., played endless games of Hearts and Spades, listened to their tapes, and remained cheerful and optimistic in their newfound recovery.

But to our dismay, John also continued to see his old drug-using friends. He just wasn't ready to give up every vestige of the old life. He dropped in regularly at a house we called Bong City. The group of college students who rented it partied continuously. *("Party" is the drug culture's verb for getting high on drugs. It has no other meaning to users. Parents need to understand this.)*

After nearly every A.A. meeting, John stopped by Bong City for a couple of hours—either testing what he was learning at A.A. or mourning his old lost life. We worried about it, but we didn't intervene.

Harlan, a user in his mid-twenties who lived at Bong City, failed to come up with his share of the rent and was kicked out. He moved back in with his parents in our neighborhood and often stopped by our house. A college drop-out and fanatic Deadhead, Harlan was now a parking-lot attendant. John spent a good bit of time with him but continued his own sober routine.

Bob and I knew Harlan's parents slightly, so we screwed up our courage and invited them to our parent support group. With the information gained there and the help of a professional intervention counselor, they planned to confront Harlan with the reality of his addiction and an ultimatum: Accept treatment and keep their support, or move out and make it on his own. They knew he was fast running out of options.

When these courageous parents enlisted the help of their son's employer, they discovered that Harlan's poor work performance was jeopardizing his job. And then they asked John to take part in the intervention. Since in times past John had gotten high with Harlan, gone to concerts with him, and knew his drugs of choice and the amounts and frequency of his using, he was in a unique position to make Harlan face the truth about his addiction.

John wrestled mightily with this issue. It was the first time he'd been called on to "work" A.A.'s Twelfth Step, in which the recovering person commits to carrying the recovery message to others. The treatment experience had shown him the necessity of confronting an active drug addict or alcoholic with the facts.

But it was hard for John to overcome old habits of covering for a fellow user, concealing the truth, denying and minimizing how often he and Harlan had gotten drunk or high or tripped together. But in the end he found the courage to participate in the intervention, along with Harlan's parents, brother, and boss. And apparently John was the most influential person there.

Harlan told him later, "Man, if you hadn't been in that room, I'd have told them all to go to hell and walked out."

Harlan's parents handed him a suitcase they'd already packed and a plane ticket for a flight leaving that same afternoon. His boss had arranged a month's leave of absence, saying that unless he accepted help immediately, he could consider himself unemployed. Harlan agreed, reluctantly, to enter the hospital.

John and Trey were also scheduled to return to the hospital—John for a six-month visit, Trey for a three-month. Harlan's parents had arranged for all three to travel together, a move that lessened their son's resistance considerably. The trio boarded the plane with their sense of humor intact; on the flight, John and Trey chipped into buy Harlan his last two beers.

At the hospital Harlan got on board wholeheartedly with the treatment program and began a beautiful recovery. In another month he too was back home, alcohol- and drug-free and grateful for John's help. As for

John, he was stronger for having overcome his fears in order to help a fellow sufferer.

John went back to work at the country club for the summer and also began to talk about a career in drug rehabilitation. Hearing of a local court-ordered program for teenaged first offenders involved with alcohol or other drugs, he volunteered to help and was accepted. In this way he could test his vocational interest and potential abilities in the field.

John's status as a recovering addict made him a powerful force for good among these troubled youngsters. Patricia, the group's professional facilitator, told him he was gifted in the work. Having a respected professional rate him as a "high-impact personality" sent his self-esteem soaring. More than once she called on him to talk with young addicts who were resisting the idea of inpatient treatment, and he found he could persuade them to accept the help they needed. His strength in his recovery was growing every day.

John, Trey, and Harlan now made an inseparable team. What Bob and I had wanted so much was finally happening. John was restructuring his life around his recovery, making new drug-free friends, discovering the natural highs he'd overlooked in his years of active addiction.

Harlan came up with an idea that fired the other two with great excitement. By far the youngest members of the local A.A. groups, all three longed for a recovery group their own age, so when Harlan proposed starting a Narcotics Anonymous chapter, John and Trey were ready to help.

The three of them pulled out all the stops to get things organized, and Middletown soon had its first N.A. meeting. John was delighted, knowing that after he returned to college his friends would have the needed support of other recovering young folks. The newly formed group grew with every meeting. Its members kept in touch between meetings as well, with picnics, fishing, tubing on the river, and N.A. dances in nearby towns.

"You know, Mom, I feel I owe myself a sort of present," John told me midway through the summer. "I'm really happy about the way my life's going, and I'm grateful to you and Dad for standing by me. Would you object if I quit work early to take a camping trip out West? I think I can save up enough money to pay for it."

"I don't see why not, if you have the money and share your plans openly. We can talk it over with Dad. But no more sneaking off to Colorado—once was enough!"

"I wouldn't sneak off, but I do want to go to Colorado again. It's so beautiful in the Rockies. This time I want it to be a natural high. And I want to take Amy along."

I hadn't expected that. As a matter of good communications I stated my feelings straightforwardly, trying to avoid any note of judgment or accusation.

"To tell the truth, John, I'm uncomfortable about your going with Amy. I think people who aren't married or deeply committed to a permanent relationship should postpone total intimacy. I wish you saw it that way too.

"But obviously you and Amy feel differently. If Amy's parents don't object, there's nothing more to say. I just wanted to state my feelings. I won't stop you from going."

"I know how you feel, Mom. I know it's not your way, and I respect your values, even if they're different from mine. And anyway, it's not just a casual thing with us. We see our relationship as special. Amy's folks know all about it. They leave Amy's choices up to her."

When John told his dad about the plan, Bob raised no objection, though he shared my reservation.

"I see no reason why not. You've been conscientious about your recovery, worked hard, lived up to your responsibilities, made healthy choices. I think you deserve it. Go on and have a wonderful time."

John chose the same destination as before, but now it was with the family's full knowledge. As he assembled the necessary camping equipment, we provided maps and a telephone credit card, got John's old car checked out, and enjoyed watching him plan his route. He said he couldn't wait to get back to the Rockies to enjoy the wilderness, the stunning scenery, the animals and wildflowers—all seen now with clear mind and keen eye, instead of through a drugged haze.

He promised to phone often to let us know his whereabouts. Trey and Harlan came around to say good-bye on the morning he was leaving to pick up Amy. Believe me, three gangling six-footers hugging and saying "I love you" loud and clear was something to behold. The affection that is so all-important to John has been a constant in his life ever since he found his way to N.A. Addicts crave affection even more than do those of us who are not chemically dependent. "Hugs are better than drugs," they say, and they really mean it. We waved John on his way, knowing how strong he was growing in his recovery and how much the trip would mean to him.

Ecstatic postcards arrived regularly, and phone calls kept us posted. Camping at ten thousand feet, with deer grazing at the edge of the campsite, was thrilling. John and Amy photographed wildflowers and animals, marveled at the clear air and soaring mountain peaks, hiked, and swam in an icy lake. At last they reluctantly made their way back East and arrived at Chambers in time for the fall quarter.

Tom was back too, well and happy and eager to start the

school year, and he and John decided to organize a campus chapter of N.A. They found a meeting place, sent away for literature, and enlisted help from nearby groups. Within a few weeks, the new chapter was off to a fine start. Tom and John were joined by half a dozen others who wanted to kick their drug dependency or maintain an ongoing recovery.

At one of the early meetings John was profoundly moved when his friend Mark, who'd had a drug problem the whole time they'd been at Chambers, asked John to be his sponsor—a special friend with recovery experience within the fellowship of N.A. Mark's recovery began in earnest that evening, and through N.A. and with the help of his Higher Power, he's been drug-free and sober ever since.

Amy had a victory too. In the Rockies she and John had talked a lot about her family, and she had realized that a beloved relative was also chemically dependent. Using knowledge gleaned from John, and with encouragement from Bob and me, Amy joined her family in planning an intervention to get the chemically dependent member into treatment. They first consulted an intervention specialist, then set up the confrontation for the Thanksgiving holiday. When the family was all assembled, they asked the problem person to hear them out as they spelled out their love and concern.

Instead of resisting, she gave in with gallant grace: "Why in the world did you wait so long?"

And so another family started down the recovery road.

When John was home for the Thanksgiving holidays, a question popped into my mind that I'd been wanting to ask. The time seemed right as we drove home together from a movie.

"You know, John, I've often wondered why you gave in so readily when I came to see you at Chambers and suggested going for treatment. What happened to break down your resistance, to make you surrender?"

He hesitated a moment. "It's something personal, Mom. I'm not sure I'm ready to share it."

"Okay, I understand. You don't have to share it if you don't want to."

He contined to mull it over. "I guess there really isn't any reason not to. When we get home, I'll write it out for you. I think I'd feel more comfortable writing it than telling it."

I had no idea what was coming. John's own words tell about his turning point much better than mine could, and the chain of events he describes go far beyond my powers of understanding:

I first tried LSD when I was fifteen years old and rapidly became enchanted with it. I loved just sitting back to enjoy the hallucinations. Sometimes the experiences were very beautiful, at other times very frightening. Most of the time they were just plain weird. I loved it all. It was a chemically induced fantasy world, and I much preferred it to the painful realities of growing up and meeting life on its own terms.

I became very good at using LSD—that is, I didn't let it shake me. Friends had bad experiences with it and shied away, but I kept coming back for more. I learned that the only way to "control" it was to surrender to it, to go with the flow, rather than fighting it.

My experiences using acid became more and more bizarre, more profound, more frightening, and, ultimately, mystical. I experienced what I perceived as visions of the divine. At times when I was tripping, I felt I was in touch with ultimate truths, seeing the unity and interconnectedness of all things. I began actively seeking that experience, which I believed was communion with

God. The use of LSD had become sacramental for me. It was the ritual act around which my spiritual life revolved. *Achieving communion with God as I understood Him, through the use of LSD, had become the focus of my life.*

On a particular day when I took a strong dose of very pure acid, I let the resultant sensations roll over me, anticipating the familiar peak experience. It never came. When I reached the summit there was nothing there. God was not there. There were no visions, no voices, no thunder or lightning—nothing. Above all, there was no communion.

It was made apparent to me, by God, through His silence, that I was way off track. The unspoken message was somehow clear: My drug use was destroying me. My spiritual quest had become perverted, and only through abstinence from all drugs would the communion be restored. At that moment I swore off all drugs forever.

In my case, "forever" lasted approximately eighteen hours, and I was stoned again. I did not yet possess the tools that I would need to stay clean. But my attitude had turned around 180 degrees. I was willing and wanting to change. I had the desire to stop using drugs, and I had an inkling that I could not do it alone.

While Sally Ann was telling me how John could find his way to wholeness, he himself was in touch with a powerful healing directive. Neither of us knew about the other's epiphany, yet we were being led to freedom at the same moment. No wonder he had tears in his eyes four days later when I showed up at Chambers. He had fully surrendered and was ready to accept our plan, because he had been unmistakably called to healing and didn't know where it was to be found. All the pieces of the puzzle were in place at last.

The rest of John's story is fairly simple. He went on to graduate from Chambers, earned a master's degree in alcohol and drug rehabilitation, and is now managing an adolescent chemical-dependency treatment program. A deeply feeling person, full of compassion and love, he has touched many lives and led numerous friends to sobriety.

Mike has had his own long struggle. A year after Family Week, I called a family conference to discuss Mike's deteriorating situation. His life was not the total chaos John's had been, but in his later high school years, he had gravitated toward the partying crowd. He barely managed to graduate, and withdrew from college in a state of great anxiety after only six weeks.

At our insistence, he went to a few counseling sessions, then let it slide. He lived at home, worked at a menial job, hung around with a crowd of potheads and heavy drinkers; he clung to the comforts of our household, though he rebelled violently against our standards. We knew he had gone back to drinking and suspected he was smoking dope again.

Bob and I were frustrated and angry, afraid we would be forced to relive our worst times all over again. Susan resented Mike's increasingly obnoxious behavior, rudeness, and hostility. John was disgusted with him and declared we had endorsed his immature behavior by allowing him to live at home and demanding nothing in return.

With their help, we set up a plan of intervention. Mike was called in and asked to listen to what we had to say. Each of us reported how frustrated and angry we felt as we described the particulars of his recent behavior—sullenness, self-centeredness, refusal to make a contribution to family life, late hours, drinking. We reminded him that all these things were danger signals for chemical dependency, and we needed an expert opinion on his case.

To his credit, Mike sat and heard us out, though he hated every minute.

Toward the end, John's sense of humor came into play. "Mike, the bottom line is, we're offering you an all-expenses-paid, four-week visit to beautiful Minnesota at the height of the winter season."

"That's right, Mike," I said. "We're asking you to go back to the hospital for a second evaluation. Last year they told you that if you couldn't stay abstinent for six months, you'd better come back for treatment. You went back to drinking after four months, and you're still doing that and smoking dope too. We have to know for certain whether you're chemically dependent."

Mike didn't deny any of it.

Susan spoke up. "Mike, this family has already suffered too much pain for far too long. It's not fair to put us through it again. It's simple, really. If the evaluation team tells you this time that you're chemically dependent, stay at the hospital for treatment. If they say you're not, then come home, grow up, and start acting like a mature human being."

Mike stared resentfully at his sister but said nothing.

Bob pressed him. "Well, son, what do you say? We're waiting for your decision. It's a good time to get this thing over with. You're not in school, you can leave your job, and you won't be missing anything important."

Mike sat in angry silence, tears glittering between his lashes.

"I have to tell you," Bob went on, "that if you refuse to go, your stuff will be moved onto the sidewalk at the end of the week. You're eighteen. You'll be on your own. We love you, but you can't live here unless you're willing to accept some help. That's our bottom line."

Mike realized we meant it. "Okay," he said with a

backed-into-a-corner sigh. "I'll go. I don't want to, and I can tell you I'm not an addict. You know I'm not. But I guess you won't be satisfied any other way. I'll be back in a week."

"Okay, Mike," said John. "We appreciate your willingness to cooperate. If they tell you you don't need to stay for treatment, you can come straight home. But if they say you do need treatment, we're asking for your word of honor that you'll stay."

"I will," said Mike. "But they won't."

He went, and he stayed a week, during which he was challenged on every side. He stuck doggedly to his contention that he wasn't an addict, in the face of tremendous pressure.

"Boy, you're really into denial big time," someone told him every day.

While we had mistaken John's addiction for a rough adolescence, we had in turn mistaken Mike's rough adolescence for addiction. In the end, a counselor phoned to tell us they were satisifed that Mike was *not* chemically dependent and didn't need treatment. But once again he was told he was a substance abuser who needed to make some hard choices about his use of chemicals. Another six-month period of abstinence was recommended.

Mike came home feeling resentful for being made to endure what he saw as an unnecessary ordeal. Bob and I made no apologies. We were entitled to know for certain whether he had the disease of chemical dependency too. Knowing he did not, we could go on to explore other areas of help for him. And no matter how he felt, he had gained many tools for practical living from that week of group therapy.

We arranged for an evaluation of his aptitudes and vocational interests, and with the renewed self-confidence this testing engendered, he decided to give college another try. He found a school that was much more congenial than the first one, and he's still there, happy and making his own unique contribution to campus life.

Mike no longer smokes dope, though he still drinks socially; but his life is coming together, and he'll get to the place he needs to be in the end. He knows he has the backing of a strong and loving family, a family that pushes him hard to share his feelings, and he has come out of his shell to risk sharing himself fully with others. Having passed unhappily through the Lost Child stage, followed by an equally unsatisfactory stab at being the Scapegoat, he's now working on the only enterprise that's likely to pay off—setting all roles aside to become a whole, mature person.

Susan's journey has been less dramatic but equally challenging. She was called into the work of healing soon after John's recovery began, when she realized that her good friend Patrick had a serious drinking problem. She confronted him with his need for help and took him to a knowledgeable counselor.

Susie and Dave are stronger people for having shared Patrick's pain. They continue to nourish their marriage and careers, and since both also have availed themselves of counseling, the quality of their lives has continually improved. Susan gratefully relinquished the role of family Hero to became just one of the gang—a much more comfortable place to be.

# CHAPTER THIRTEEN

# Cutting In the Afterburner

————*R*ecovery is for everyone in the family—not just the addict. John was on his way, Susie had her own life to live, Mike was settling in at college, and Bob had his work. Suddenly my editorial work no longer seemed meaningful, and I was also facing the empty-nest syndrome. All that energy previously focused on John and his problem had to be rechannelled in healthier directions. Where to begin?

From the earliest days of our marriage I had been subject to bouts of depression. Bob wanted to help in these bad times, but the problem was beyond us both. As a rule I simply endured the depression and waited stoically for the eventual lifting of the black cloud.

During one such miserable spell in our first year together, Bob had tried to comfort me.

"Honey, I'm making you a promise right now," he said tenderly. "Just as soon as I can afford it—"

What was he promising? Jewels, furs, trips around the world? The suspense was brief.

"Just as soon as I can afford it," he repeated, "I'm lining you up with the *best psychiatrist money can buy!*"

Well . . . I ask you, what woman wants to be told she

needs a psychiatrist? I was insulted and hurt. Later it became a family joke, but now years later, the idea cropped up again. John's recovery had not created the steady state of happiness I had expected. I was still depressed and showed no sign of snapping out of it.

I had read about the work of the pioneering psychotherapist Carl Jung. His teachings struck me as wholly sympathetic, and I wondered whether such therapy might help me break free of my depression. At the height of my misery a woman trained in the Jungian method arrived in Middletown. It was too much of a coincidence to ignore. With Bob's encouragement, I met with her to discuss long-term therapy. The chemistry between us felt right, and after several exploratory sessions we committed ourselves to the awesome undertaking of long-term depth analysis.

By no means did I consider myself mentally ill. I thought of analysis as a gift I was giving myself—a personal enrichment, a psychic adornment. It proved to be far more, and the eventual rewards far surpassed those meager early expectations.

Legions of dreams obediently presented themselves night after night as I began to work with Kate. I recorded them faithfully and brought them in each week to be held up to the light of mutual exploration. The necessary trust between us was not built overnight, but was achieved gradually. Kate understood me, accepted me unconditionally, and asked only a totally unguarded sharing of my thoughts and dreams. Affirming my uniqueness, Kate was the friend I needed.

With the progress of the analytic work came additional opportunities for growth. Bob and I attended a conference led by John Sanford, a prominent Jungian therapist and writer. The gathering took place at a mountain retreat beside a serene lake; the colors of the autumn woods alone would have made the trip worthwhile. Attended by a sympathetic and interesting mix of people, this conference stirred deep directions of change for us both.

John Sanford spoke movingly of the power of dreams and stories to bring about individuation—the divine birthright of uniqueness, which already is ours if we will only claim it. Several times during the conference mention was made of spiritual direction, and since my analytic work was bringing up spiritual issues, I gathered names and addresses of persons who might be helpful in this connection. Bob was impressed by what he learned about dreams and personality type.

This memorable weekend was our first carefree time together in years. We had stopped focusing on John, and in consequence, our own spirits were flourishing. Refreshed and rejuvenated, we continued to draw upon this new surge of energy.

Back home, I had the sudden and bewildering experience of being unable to understand any piece of writing that was not spiritually oriented. I could only obey this peculiar inner dictate and confine my reading to those books that made sense to me: *The Way of a Pilgrim,* (translated from the Russian); *Behold the Spirit* by Alan Watts; John Sanford's *The Kingdom Within;* Donald Nicholl's *Holiness;* and Thomas Merton's *Seven Storey Mountain,* to name just a few. Each spoke to a deep and mysterious hunger.

Bob continued his study of personality type along Jungian lines and found it explained a great deal about interpersonal relations both within and beyond our family. As his understanding and respect for their power grew, he too began to record his dreams and ponder them, harking back to Family Week and his life-changing dream of the brain that had to be cut through to reach the heart.

As these complex and curious currents took shape in our lives, Kate injected a new component into my analysis—body work. Negation of everything physical was one of my chief emotional defenses. I was sedentary, overweight, and hypertensive. Sexual expression was a matter of the dullest routine, the intensity of desire having become lost somewhere along the way. It was time to give up treating my physical self as an adversary and rediscover the vital body I remembered from my childhood.

I had no idea how to carry out spontaneous movement, even to music. I assumed there was some "right" way to do it and relied mainly on Kate's direction. Carefully, gently, gradually, she led me to rediscover my body, pay attention to its messages, think myself into all parts of it rather than sealing off my awareness inside my brain-box's ivory tower.

With time and practice, movement became more free and a more consistent awareness of bodily tensions emerged. As I learned to identify such tension, I learned to manage it. For example, when I stretched out on the floor, closed my eyes, breathed slowly and steadily, and relaxed as deeply as possible, I could release that tension.

Accumulated physical strain had been an unsuspected and constant burden on my body. When I learned to recognize and deal with it, I was far more comfortable from day to day. By practicing thorough relaxation, I could even get rid of a headache or backache without resorting to medication.

After what seemed like weeks of waiting, one of my inquiries about spiritual direction was answered. A priest in a neighboring parish was trained in this ministry, and I could scarcely wait to call him. No longer trying to manage everything on my own, I reached out eagerly for help.

When I spoke with Father Matthew, he understood what I sought better than I understood it myself. His voice over the phone was resonant, warm, encouraging. True to pattern, a dream prepared me for our first meeting.

By now I accepted without question the direction of my Higher Power that so often came in dreams. These no longer seemed strange or alien but were uniquely personal interior dramas, sometimes cheerful and amusing, sometimes darkly powerful, each having deep roots in my day-to-day life. Drawing from both light and dark sides of myself, the dreams were highly charged reflections of the new ways into which life was leading me, and also of the obstacles to be surmounted.

In the dream that preceded my first meeting with Father Matthew, I drove across a mountain (something I actually would do) and arrived at a medieval hospice run by monks. This hospice, built of stone, stood beside the pits from which the stone had been quarried. The monk who received me was kind and comforting. Although I understood that the hospice was not my final goal, I settled in gratefully for the time being, confident that I could rest there before taking up my journey again.

This dream boded well for the work with Father Matthew. Stone is imperishable, after all, the eternal bedrock on which the world is founded. In calling upon such a spiritual caregiver, I would be drawing upon something secure and lasting. My clearest association was with Jesus' parable of the foolish man who built his house upon sand and the wiser one who established his upon solid rock. Although I didn't realize it at the time, the dream was telling me that this spiritual friendship was to be a temporary resting place rather than a permanent haven.

Many outside demands were made on my time during this period. Other Middletown parents caught in the struggle with drug- and alcohol-abusing teens had heard about our family's success and were hungry for help. We were more than willing to give it, so our parent support group continued to be a first priority. We invested considerable time and effort in sharing the message of hope that had meant so much to us.

This effort was both rewarding and exhausting. Listening as other suffering parents recounted their pain brought back much of our own. Time and again, another parent's account of walking the floor until 3:00 A.M., going to court with an antisocial teenager, or withstanding a barrage of drunken profanity brought fresh tears to our eyes. As we shared the agony with others, we felt intensely grateful for our own delivery from such turmoil, privileged to be helping someone else.

As this outreach grew I came to regard it as a ministry of sorts, and my editorial work seemed less and less important. As a writer, I yearned desperately for a creative life I could call my own, but I also felt strongly that God was directing me to reach out to others caught in the spiral of addiction. Eventually I found an answer that accommodated both imperatives. I gave up my editorial work and resolved to begin writing my own story. Bob bought a word processor to make my task easier, and this book is the fruit of that resolve.

At my first session with Father Matthew I shared both my ambition to tell my family's story and my deep-seated fear of literary failure, manifesting the low self-esteem so common in dysfunctional families.

"We already know you can write," my mentor said. "This biographical sketch you brought me is interesting, well expressed, rich in substance. You *are* a writer."

"But suppose I write the book and it doesn't succeed."

"What's the worst thing that can happen?"

"Everyone will know I failed, and I'll feel awful."

"Can you handle that?"

"It doesn't sound unbearable, does it?"

"It doesn't to me. What about you?"

"I suppose I'll never know I can succeed unless I'm willing to try."

"Trust yourself, Betsy." Father Matthew's kind expression seconded his encouraging words. "Remember that anyone who creates a work of art, regardless of how it's received, is a participant in the Divine Creation."

"I never thought of it like that. If you believe in me, I guess I'll have to believe in myself."

But my voice trembled and my palms were sweaty. I wished I could feel as confident about the undertaking as he seemed to be.

"Now one thing will be *very* important in our work together," Father Matthew went on. "I want you to begin keeping to a rule of life. By this I mean to arrange a certain order in your days—a regular time for getting up, a time for prayer, a time for work, a time for exercise, a time for recreation. The prayer time is particularly important. In the beginning it will be difficult, because it generally takes at least thirty days to form a habit. If you pray without fail for at least twenty minutes each day, a month from now, that quiet time will have become a comfortable and regular part of your life. Are you willing to commit to the effort?"

"I'll do whatever you think is right for me."

"That's good, Betsy. Living by a rule will make it easier for you to write, too. I want you to start by keeping a journal of your prayer experience. Write down every day how you went about praying, what it felt like, what came about. Bring the journal in next month, and we'll talk about it then."

So two new disciplines entered my life: I set aside a half-hour every morning for prayer and meditation, and I wrote for a major portion of each day. I began to say no to most outside activities. I bought a telephone answering machine. I got up on schedule and kept my prayer time on schedule. I sat down at my word processor at the same time every day and wrote, whether I felt like it or not. And all the while, we continued our parent support group.

A third effort, sporadic at first, had to do with exercise. Both Father Matthew and Kate wisely counseled regular exercise—a natural corollary to body work. Both urged me to choose an activity I could and would do faithfully. The least unpleasant one I could think of was walking. It was a good choice, since it required only a pair of comfortable shoes. I could walk on whatever schedule suited me, alone or with someone else, and in nearly all weathers, although I drew the line at downpours of rain.

The first few months, I huffed and puffed a bare half mile and soaked in a tub of hot water afterward to ease my aching muscles. Gradually I worked up to a mile, then two. I started to enjoy my day's jaunt, striding along without considering the effort. My breathing became easier. I enjoyed the cloud patterns, signs of the changing seasons, songs of the birds, and meeting other walkers and friendly dogs. After several months, walking became pleasure instead of a chore.

My morning meditation also took on a pattern. At first I

followed a set reading or prayer, pondered it quietly, and concluded with spontaneous silent prayer. By degrees I was able to do without the set formula and sat quietly, my mind open and waiting. When distractions came, I ceased struggling against them, and eventually they faded or passed by. Over time, my body became comfortable with this period of quietness and confident relaxation, and I could sit quite still for a full half hour. Invariably at the end, I was calmer and more serene, ready for the day in a new and different way—not supercharged with adrenaline, as in the past, but quietly alert, in touch with a more profound energy.

Now, the things I have done to make my own life fuller and richer may not be things others will find fulfilling. Each of us is a distinct individual, with various talents and needs. The key to fulfillment lies in learning to know and appreciate one's own unique, God-given self, and to adhere to whatever path is right for that self.

All my life I have been aware of a spiritual inclination; now I began to actively nourish that inclination. I have always enjoyed the imaginative world of stories and dreams; now I began to create stories and cherish dreams. I have accepted the reality that I am essentially an intuitive, introverted person, happiest away from crowds and confusion, and have learned to savor the rich stillness of ordered life, prayerful solitude, and writing. And as I worked to strengthen my less-developed physical side, it gave balance to all the rest.

Only you can discover what will lend richness to your own journey—through self-examination, trial and error, and trusting to those impulses that call forth your most positive energies and bring about the greatest inner peace. Joseph Campbell, the great scholar of myth, taught that by following our bliss, we invariably discover that doors which before were fast closed will begin to swing open. To find out who we are, and then to grow into that unique person—this is the paramount task of life.

The effects of the disciplined life, under the tutelage of Father Matthew, were extraordinary. During part of that time I kept a prayer journal, as well as continuing with my writing. I felt grounded in a creative energy far greater than my own limited powers. At times the words fairly leaped onto the screen, coming to me faster than I could type. I *was* participating in the Divine Creation! On days when the writing went swiftly and well, I was quietly joyous, grateful for new energy, knowing I was creating something truly my own. On days when I did not write for one reason or another, I was restless and edgy, aware that something vital was missing.

My prayer life was generally intense, and I had several experiences which I reluctantly labeled visions. Father Matthew counseled me to attach little importance to these experiences; they mattered less than my faithfulness to daily prayer and an attitude of receptivity. After some months I began to keep a second period of quiet in the late afternoon, when my energies were at their lowest ebb; this relaxed and refreshed me for the activities of the coming evening.

I stepped up my walking until four, five, even six miles came easily. I had more energy than I'd ever had in my life and needed far less sleep. For the first time, the thought of an afternoon nap seemed ridiculous. And oddly enough, I no longer enjoyed alcohol in any form—beer gave me a headache, liquor depressed me and made my heart race, and if I drank wine in the early evening, I was awake at

1:00 or 2:00 in the morning with the sensation of being in a sauna.

When I reported this odd development, Father Matthew said, "God is purifying you for something, Betsy. I'm not sure what it is, but I'm not surprised. Anybody who has prayed as hard as you have is bound to experience startling changes."

One fine day, I realized that my penchant for profanity, which had been with me since adolescence and also had been taken up by John in his addicted days, had simply evaporated. As I came to accept myself fully, I no longer needed this "crutch." The change arose from no bidding or effort of my own but rather from a deep impulse of inner cleansing.

A further change had to do with my weight. I began to think of doing something about my obesity. In our parent support group I had seen at first hand the power of the Twelve Steps, a recovery program originating in Alcoholics Anonymous and now used by many other recovery groups. People in torment can achieve wonderful things through the Twelve Steps—lasting sobriety, an awe-inspiring peace of mind. Why not apply the Steps to my weight problem?

I looked up the local chapter of a Twelve-Step overeaters' group and resolved to attend the next meeting. Afraid I'd back out at the last minute, I told no one of my plan: *If it works, they'll find out later on.* That meeting was the right place for me. Only a few members were present, but they welcomed me with genuine love and understanding. I was finally ready to admit the need for help with my own addiction, after spending such a long time concentrating on John's.

*Compulsive eating* is the name of my particular disorder. Rather than eating in response to physical hunger, compulsive eaters use food for emotional comfort or for pleasure. My eating was as much out of control as John's use of alcohol and other drugs had been. I never knew whether I could eat one cookie and stop, or go on to eat the entire bagful. Every time I visited Susan, I made sweeping forays through the supermarket, like Lady Bountiful, to fill up her refrigerator. I was behaving exactly like an alcoholic, except that instead of storing up six-packs of beer or half-gallons of vodka, I stored up doughnuts, ice cream, cookies.

I felt ashamed when I realized how greedy I must have appeared to others. Weighing in at well over two hundred, I had been eating compulsively most of my life. I nibbled all day as I prepared meals. I looked forward to every meal and every occasion for a snack. My chief concern about traveling was where and how well I would eat.

Kate had listened patiently throughout many of our sessions as I complained of being unable to lose weight. I rationalized, minimized, laughed it off, changed the subject—all the defenses, in fact, that addicts use. A foodaholic, I was a stereotype of addictive thinking and behavior.

Kate must have grown pretty tired of it after so long, for one day she commented with a knowing smile, "It's an odd thing, Betsy. Do you know, there were *no* fat people in the concentration camps!"

Kate's remark really sank in. It's so simple: When you can't overeat, you don't get fat. My problem was *not* a peculiar metabolism, a glandular condition, or some rare inherited tendency, as I had tried to tell myself. I was stuffing my face with more calories than I was burning up, and as long as I kept doing it, I would get fatter and fatter.

The compulsive eaters' group was my main support

over the next several months. I continued to walk, and a sensible eating program helped me shed the pounds: three well-balanced moderate meals every day, no sugar or refined flour, very little fat and only lean meats, lots of fresh vegetables and fruits. I quit nibbling and snacking between meals. *There was no magic formula.* I just began to eat in a healthy way, for life and strength, rather than to meet neurotic needs.

As I slimmed down, acquaintances stopped me on the street and in the supermarket to tell me how great I looked. Each compliment encouraged me. Most weeks, I lost at least two pounds, sometimes more. After the first week, the bothersome hunger pains disappeared; my body was adjusting to the new way of life.

New clothes became necessary when the old ones could be altered no further. From my new point of view, my old wardrobe was astonishingly drab and dreary. For years I'd worn black, grey, and navy, hoping to blend into the background. How depressed I had been, and how long it had lasted! The new me craved bright-colored clothes: brilliant blues, lively reds, throbbing purples. The energy stirring on the inside had to find its way out.

My doctor was surprised on my next regular visit to see me considerably thinner and with a normal blood pressure.

"What have you been up to?"

"Oh, not much—just working with an analyst, seeing a spiritual director, meditating regularly, eating right, and walking for exercise."

"Obviously it's a powerful combination! You look great, and your blood pressure is right where it should be. How would you feel about a trial period off your medication?"

A month later my blood pressure was still normal, and again a month after that. I exulted in being free of pills, although my weight crept up a bit as my body adjusted to its new chemical balance.

As my physical energies grew and my body changed, disturbing new thoughts began to surface, and finally I admitted to myself that the sexual relationship between Bob and me was very unhealthy. It had never been great, but in recent years I had lost all interest in physical affection. We both harbored smoldering resentments: Bob wanted satisfaction of his sexual needs, and I seemed to have none.

We had resigned ourself to this state of affairs, exactly as we had resigned ourselves to John's sick behavior. This comparison struck me along with a solution to our dilemma. When we had learned what was wrong with John, we sought the best specialized help we could find. Why not seek out the best help available for our sexual problems?

One day when Bob came home from work I told him what I'd been thinking and timidly suggested asking for an appointment at a well-known clinic for sexual dysfunctions.

He jumped at my suggestion. "Why didn't I think of that myself?" He grabbed the telephone book and started looking up long-distance codes.

I was shyly jubilant. Surely it wasn't too late, as long as we both were willing to try. All these years he and I had stood by each other, faithfully living out our marriage covenant—sometimes in grim determination, sometimes in anguish, only once in a while in a very mild transport of pleasure. We respected and loved each other deeply, but we never had attained the level of delight that inspires the poets. Could we hope for such a thing now, in our settled years? Could we learn to play thrilling new tunes upon our lumpy middle-aged bodies?

Our inquiry brought a positive response from the clinic. We were accepted into the program and a date was set for our initial interview. Our therapy would extend over a period of two weeks. We were to stay in a nearby hotel and visit the clinic each day.

Having never spent two weeks in a hotel with Bob, I wondered how we would amuse ourselves during all that time! It turned out to be the honeymoon we had never had, the idyllic vacation away from family cares that we'd often dreamed of but never realized.

Our therapists at the clinic were personable, intelligent, and thoroughly competent. Great care was taken to keep the relationship professional; we were always addressed as Dr. and Mrs., and we always used their professional titles. Total confidentiality was maintained; throughout our two weeks, we never glimpsed another patient or therapist.

After the initial psychological testing and history taking, the basic building blocks of any good relationship—*feelings* and *communication*—were addressed. We nodded smugly.

"We know all about communication and dealing with feelings," I told our team. "We learned that during Family Week at the hospital with John."

"Can you describe what you learned?"

"Well, I might say to John, 'When I'm talking to you and you stare silently out the window with a cold expression, I feel left out and rejected.'"

"Good! You can obviously identify feelings and talk about them. That's a major achievement in itself. Sometimes people are here a week or more before they understand what a feeling is.

"You reported what happened and its emotional effect on you. But here we add a third step. We would say, 'When you stare out the window, I feel rejected. *What I need from you* is to look at me so I'll know you haven't shut me out, and to respond in some way that will let me know what you're thinking.' "

Bob caught on right away.

"I get it. I might say to Betsy, 'You're reading a book, and I'm feeling lonely. I'd like you to put down your book and sit by me for a few minutes, so I can feel we're really together.' "

"You've got it," the therapist said. "We'd like you both to practice doing that all day, every day, as long as you're here. Get in touch with your own feelings, identify them, and state them as clearly as you can. Then *let the other person know* what you need or want. Of course, the other person can choose how to respond. We'll get to that later."

Our hardest task was to learn to use "I" language. Our therapists taught us the all-importance of being able to say "I need . . ." or "I want . . ."; it doesn't sound difficult, but for us it was a colossal undertaking.

Our entire lives had been built around a counterproductive communication system, summarized by the phrase, "Would you like . . . ?" From earliest childhood, we had been taught to put other people's needs first. In both our families, "I need . . . " or "I want . . . " was viewed as rude and selfish. It was better to be pleasant than candid, better to give in than insist, more Christian to submit than to stand pat. We knew no other way to communicate.

Such a system is doubly flawed. First, the person questioned must read the mind of the questioner. And the questioner is so concerned about the other's response, all sense of his or her own needs and wants is lost.

We practiced simple examples of "I" language every day: "I'm feeling hungry and I'd like a snack. I need to know how you feel about that"; "I'd like to look in the shop windows on the other side of the street, which means we have to cross at this corner. I need to check that out with you."

It sounds silly, but when we realized how difficult it was for us to carry out these simple exchanges, we knew we needed to learn. We gained additional communication skills: how to negotiate differences of opinion and, when our needs differed, how to decide whose need was greater.

Once we learned to *talk* effectively to each other, we needed to move beyond the shutting-down of feelings that had pervaded our family during John's illness. As we became better at communicating feelings, needs, and wants, our therapists helped us use this new skill in gentle, gradual rediscovery of our natural sexual energies.

At the end of each daily clinic session, we were given a task to carry out in the privacy of our hotel room. These tasks constituted a graded and careful progression of physical togetherness, which respected the bounds of emotional comfort for both and was surprisingly similar to courtships in the horse-and-buggy days. No step was taken until both partners desired and assented to it fully, whether it was an early one, such as simply stroking the partner's hand, or, near the end, the fullest genital connection. Suspense was built into the process. Throughout, both partners expressed their own needs and wants.

Responsibility—*response-ability*—was the goal. As we no longer shut down our feelings when they began to be uncomfortable, but managed them in a new way, we regained the ability to respond to each other creatively, which released much new energy for us both.

In our free time during those two weeks we explored a new city's attractions: parks, museums, shops, and restaurants. We went for a long walk every day in the park and held hands like teenagers. In the art museum, we kissed behind the exhibits. Bob bought me a beautiful new dress and necklace; I felt like a queen. I bought the handsome dressing-gown he had admired in a store window, and he preened in it like a peacock.

One evening during the second week as we lingered over a candlelight dinner, our smiling young waitress surprised us with a question: "I hope you don't mind my asking, but have you folks just recently gotten married?"

We burst out laughing.

"Not very recently," said Bob through his chuckles. "Actually, it was almost thirty years ago. Why did you think we were newlyweds?"

"You were leaning across the table, talking to each other in such a romantic way and holding hands, I figured you had to be newlyweds. Old married people just don't act like that!"

We really did feel like newlyweds; it must have been sticking out all over us. Strangers frequently stared at us with fascination. *You look happy,* their expressions seemed to say, *and we'd like some of it too.*

Getting our marriage back on track was a benediction for the rest of the family. Susan could finally stop worrying about us. Within a few months she and Dave delightedly informed us we were to become grandparents. They were free at last to commit their energies to the next generation. Both were aware that they might have a chemically dependent youngster some day, but they felt prepared to face that challenge when and if it came.

John confessed he had often wondered whether Bob and I might divorce; he was thankful to see there was no chance of it. He and Amy had struggled with the issue of whether to make their relationship permanent. After several emotional ups and downs, they sought the help of a counselor and soon decided they were ready for a lifelong commitment. Amy loved John steadfastly and had stuck by him through thick and thin. It was good to see these two strong, deeply caring young people pledge their lives and love.

The most surprising result of the healing of our marriage had to do with Mike, who always kept his feelings to himself, who couldn't let anyone know he cared—self-sufficient Mike, who prided himself on being cool. At eighteen, for the first time in his life, Mike was able to say "I love you." We felt like shouting. Mike still grins every time he says "I love you" to one of us, happy to be a full-fledged member of the tribe at last.

For us, the smoke screen had vanished, and the awakening had truly begun.

# CHAPTER FOURTEEN

# A Plan of Action for You

__N__ow for a very personal word to you, the reader: If you've known the pain of substance abuse or chemical dependency in your family, take heart from our family's story. By claiming your courage, you can begin today to sweep away the cobwebs of helplessness and despair. No matter how discouraging your situation, things *can* change. You may not be able to change the person you're concerned about, but *you can change yourself and your reactions to that person.* And when any one element in a situation changes, the other elements must adjust to that change.

The approach to family recovery which follows is based on my own experience and the resources I have found useful; the appended reading list offers additional help. If you follow these suggestions carefully and conscientiously, your life situation *will* change for the better. The chemical battle is not won overnight, but it is never lost, as long as even *one* person in a family is willing to change.

Right now you probably feel bewildered and helpless, not knowing what to do or where to start. Those feelings are very real. You can't rid yourself of them. You can only feel them, then go on through them to productive action.

With a step-by-step approach, you *can* begin to change things. Don't try to tackle everything at once. Just take one thing at a time, and be good to yourself in the process. Are you ready? Okay—take a deep breath. Here we go!

1. Get the focus off the substance abuser and onto yourself. Catalog the facts of *your* situation. Take a realistic look at *your* life and how *you* are living it. What part are *you* playing in the drama? What are *your* habitual reactions to the problem person?

To get started, take pencil and paper and jot down your answers to the following questions. (If appropriate, substitute "she" or "he" and "him" or "her.") Do you:

—House and feed an alcohol/drug abuser but expect nothing in return?
—Endure inconsiderate or abusive behavior, thinking you have no other choice?
—Put up with the user's infantile dependency, for fear he can't make it alone in the Big World?
—Stay home in order to control the abuser's behavior?
—Stay away from home to avoid scenes and hurt?
—Provide an automobile and insurance for someone who is a terrible driving risk?
—Provide a key to your home so she is free to come and go at all hours?
—Make excuses to the school, the boss, relatives and friends?
—Lose sleep wondering where he is?
—Find yourself obsessed with her behavior?
—Get calls in the middle of the night from the police, the hospital, irate parents, or strangers who refuse to identify themselves?
—Believe your abuser would be all right if it were not for his undesirable friends?

—Cover the user's bad checks or pay off her debts?

—Say nothing when valuables are missing, alcohol disappears from your private store, drugs vanish from your medicine cabinet?

—Shield the abuser from painful consequences of his behavior, such as jail, expulsion from school, or getting fired?

—Nag, preach, plead, and cry, to no avail?

—Live in constant fear of what might happen to her, or what she might do to you or to others?

—Blame yourself and believe it must all be your fault or the fault of other family members?

—Conceal unpleasant facts from other members of the family?

—Neglect your own health, emotional needs, appearance, recreation, or social life?

If you answered Yes to more than one of these questions, your situation is indeed unhappy. If you gave four or five Yes responses, you are living by an unacceptable set of rules, and it's time for a change.

"What's the use?" you're probably thinking. "I've tried everything, and nothing changes."

You may have tried every way you know to control and change your problem person, but that never works. The more you try to control an addict, the more control he or she gains over *you.* It doesn't matter right now whether your user is ready to change or not. *Forget about the user for the moment, and concentrate on yourself.*

You need not settle for life on terms set by an addict. You can make your own terms, reclaim responsibility for yourself and your own life, in spite of others' refusal to assume responsibility for theirs. You can change your own reactions, beginning today.

If you're already hurting so much that you know things must change, go on to 2.

2. Make a list of the things you can change, and start to change them, one by one. Go back to 1, above. For every Yes answer you gave, consider some other possibilities:

—If your fifteen-year-old refuses to put the necessary effort into school assignments or plays truant, you can stop picking up the slack and let her face the music.

—If your sixteen-year-old exhibits destructive, erratic, and irresponsible behavior, as parent or legal guardian, you can withhold consent for a driver's permit and use of your car. Your state's department that deals with licenses will support you in your stand.

—If your seventeen-year-old won't keep his curfew, you can take away his key or have the locks changed, lock the door at a certain hour, go to bed (even if you have to use earplugs), and let him sleep in the shrubbery.

—If your eighteen-year-old habitually sponges on the rest of the family and makes no contribution, you can stop being a sucker for her pleas for support.

—If your nineteen-year-old is arrested for drunk driving, you can let him spend the night in jail and arrange his own defense.

—If your twenty-five-year-old continues to live at home and depend on you financially, you can tell her to make other arrangements, give her a deadline, and if she hasn't left when that day arrives, put her things on the curb and enlist the aid of the police to make it stick.

—If you've concealed troublesome knowledge from other family members, you can tell everyone you think there's a serious problem and ask them to sit down together to pool information.

This radically different way of thinking and acting will take some getting used to. At first, guilt may get in your way. You may feel like a heartless person. Don't let this temptation trip you up. Something *must* change, and the first step is up to *you*. A human doormat serves no one's long-term good.

Here's the cardinal rule for dealing with a substance abuser: *Only when the consequences of the destructive behavior become sufficiently painful will an addict see any reason to change.* By allowing a person to suffer the predictable consequences of irresponsible behavior, you move an abuser that much closer to recovery.

But the most important result of the change in your reactions will be the boost to your *own* self-esteem. Having been a doormat for so long, when you reclaim your power of personal choice, you will feel a surge of vital new energy. *Help yourself first.* After that, you may be able to help someone else.

There are no hard-and-fast rules to guide you in the first stages of attitude adjustment, but there is a general process that will help.

First of all, *calm yourself* in whatever way works for you—other than using alcohol or other drugs. You don't want to fall into the same trap as the person you're concerned about. Do some deep breathing. Practice total body relaxation. Take a warm, soothing bubble bath. Go for a long walk, meditate, take a swim, anything that helps you relax. While your emotions rage, your mind cannot do its best work. Most people know what's right for them and can find a solution, once they become calm enough.

*Look at the facts clearly.* It may be helpful to use pencil and paper to describe what's going on, as though you were writing up your family life for a true-confessions magazine. No one will read it but you, so tell it like it is. When you see your predicament spelled out in black and white, you are better able to put changes into place that will serve your family's long-range health and wholeness.

*Set realistic goals.* If you know in your heart that you have the guts to change just one tiny thing and will stick to it, start with that one tiny thing, then build on it later as you gain confidence. One successful change will give you courage to make others.

*A united family front is essential.* Enlist the help of all family members, especially the other parent. Do not allow your child to play one parent against another, or use a sibling or other relative as an ally against parental exercise of responsibility. Even divorced parents can stand together when they understand that their child's survival is at stake. Nor should any helping professional be permitted to ally with a child against a parent. If this happens, find a new counselor right away—one who understands that teamwork by all players is crucial. You can usually secure this essential cooperation if you identify the issue as a life-and-death concern.

*Be consistent—say what you mean, and mean what you say.* Avoid making threats. Your youngster has already heard threats that you haven't been able to carry out. When the abuser realizes you intend to hold your ground on a single issue, no matter how small, he or she will begin to take you seriously. Consequences are not the same as threats. Consequences are necessary; threats are empty. *Spell out clearly the consequences of irresponsible behavior; then let them happen.*

3. Find out about support groups in your community and start attending one or more. Helpful groups include Families Anonymous, Al-Anon, and Nar-

Anon. Your local information-referral service or crisis line should be able to put you in touch with chapters in your area.

Once you attend a meeting and see how many other decent, caring parents are up against the same problem, you will stop feeling so terribly alone.

*Admit your need and ask for help.* When I started to tell people that my son had a drug problem, help began to come. You can find fellow pilgrims wherever you may be.

*Keep on attending your support group, and encourage other family members to attend,* even if the first few meetings aren't particularly thrilling. Stick with your group and work its program faithfully; over the long haul, it will be your most important resource.

Some people go to support groups looking for a quick fix, then drop out in disillusionment when they don't find it. *There is no quick fix in chemical dependency.* The road to recovery is a long one, and it calls for hard work on the part of everyone affected. But the journey can be greatly enhanced by the understanding and loving support of others who have been down that road before you.

*Identify individuals in the support group with whom you feel particularly comfortable and talk with them after and between meetings.* Some groups call such friends *sponsors.* Such friendships can mean a great deal on both the rough and the sunny days—a great combination of compassionate concern and practical experience.

If you cannot locate a support group in your area, write for literature and start a group yourself. The most helpful group I have found for parents of substance abusers is Families Anonymous (14553 Delano Street, Suite 316, Van Nuys, CA 91411; telephone 818/989-7985). Just two or three dedicated persons can build a thoroughly

effective group. It takes time, but it's well worth the
investment.

4. Get help for yourself from a qualified professional
   who understands substance abuse and what it does
   to a family. You can break up the destructive cycle
   by working on your own personal program of
   growth. You, the nonaddicted person, *must* learn to
   be in control of yourself. A skillful, impartial
   counselor can help you take stock of how you're
   doing and lead you into healthier ways of living,
   complementing the help of your support group.
   Money need not be a problem. Many communities
   have counselors who will work out sliding-scale
   payments for those who cannot afford the usual fee.

If, after some time with a particular counselor, you can't
shake the feeling that he or she is not really helping, trust
your instincts and find someone else. I felt that way when
our family was meeting with the people at the Substance
Abuse Center. We were wasting time and money, and
better help was available elsewhere. Not all counseling
professionals are good ones; second- and third-rate
ignorant and uninformed folks exist in every field. If you
encounter a counselor who's not helping, don't be
embarrassed to call it quits and try again. It's your life! Look
for someone with the knowledge and ability you need.

5. Learn everything you can about substance abuse,
   chemical dependency, alcoholism, addiction, and
   dysfunctional families. Knowledge is power! As you
   accumulate facts, you will better understand the
   reality you're dealing with. When you put your
   reason and intelligence to work, you overcome three
   obstacles—ignorance, panic, and helplessness.

Support groups such as Al-Anon and Families Anonymous provide a wide array of helpful literature at modest cost. The appended reading list includes a good basic references. Try your public library, community mental-health agency, substance-abuse council, and alcohol/drug treatments centers for additional up-to-date information.

6. Let the problem person know you are seeking help. What to say? "I think our whole family is in trouble, and I'm doing my part to make things better." If questions persist, try this: "I'm beginning to think a disease called chemical dependency may be at the root of our family's difficulties. I'm trying to learn all I can about it." That's food for thought!

*Resist the temptation to blame or accuse.* Keep cool. Be patient and courteous, and emphasize that you are the one who needs help. In many families, once parents discover the recovery tools and make use of them in day-to-day life, an adolescent or young-adult abuser also will move into recovery. Adults who reach out to help themselves are models for their youngsters.

7. Accept the likelihood that your problem person may be suffering from a treatable disease. Chemical dependency is recognized by health professionals as a bona-fide illness. It is also a *primary* disease. This means that it must be dealt with *first,* before its accompanying disturbances—physical illness, emotional problems, family turmoil—can be helped. If chemical dependency is the problem, it will not go away, and in the absence of intervention, things *will* get progressively worse.

How can you know whether your child is in fact

chemically dependent? A formal chemical-dependency evaluation, conducted by experienced substance-abuse professionals, is the only way to know for certain. Parents cannot make this diagnosis. Eventually, you will need to settle the question. Until then, *keep before you the possibility that your child may be drinking and drugging because he or she cannot help it.* An addict's drinking or drug taking is neither a hostile action directed at the family, nor a sign of a weak character. The chemically dependent person of any age drinks or uses drugs because of an overwhelming compulsion to do so.

Whether the problem is true chemical dependency, substance abuse, or behavioral acting-out, the same rules apply. When drinking and drugging cause family problems, that family needs help. The true nature of the difficulty eventually will become clear, but until it does, you should assume you are dealing with a disease.

8. Investigate treatment programs. If your child is alcoholic or addicted to other drugs (no matter how desperately you'd like to believe otherwise), he or she will need the help of professionals. *Diseases require treatment.* Most areas of the country now have treatment facilities which employ well-qualified substance-abuse specialists.

Regardless of whether you're ready to make a decision about treatment, begin to explore and accumulate information, laying the groundwork. Make contact with every chemical-dependency treatment program you hear of and keep a file on each one.

What should you look for in a treatment facility?

—A no-obligation exploratory conference for parents or other concerned family members.

—A formal chemical-dependency evaluation, carried out by experienced substance-abuse professionals—preferably recovering abusers. If your problem person is not addicted, you'll find out at this point.

—A staff with a majority of recovering chemically dependent persons.

—An environment free of mind-altering drugs. A chemically dependent person cannot get well on a steady diet of Valium.

—Orientation of the treatment program to the principles of Alcoholics Anonymous and Narcotics Anonymous, with maximum participation in A.A. and N.A. during both acute-phase treatment and aftercare.

—A strong and intensive family program which emphasizes Twelve-Step recovery programs (Al-Anon, Nar-Anon, Families Anonymous).

—Ongoing aftercare for the chemically dependent person *and all other family members*.

—For teenage substance abusers, a proven track record in the treatment of adolescents. Caring for addicted youngsters is a demanding and highly specialized task.

This is the time to look into your medical insurance coverage. The money may not need to come out of your own pocket. Many third-party payers now cover all or most of the cost of chemical-dependency treatment. Most treatment facilities also have some "indigent beds" for those with no financial resources, and some have endowments to assist those who cannot pay. State funds may be available. Don't hesitate to ask about financial aspects.

If the cost seems high, how much is your child's life worth? The price of a new car? The cost of a year of

college? *The lives of young people are priceless! Keep
things in proportion.*

A strong personal prejudice must be stated here. I
believe that both treatment based on a traditional
psychiatric model, and treatment in a strongly sectarian
religious program are apt to fail. Programs of either type
can do more harm than good. If people go through such a
program without any benefit from it, they are likely to
conclude there is no such thing as good treatment, thus
cutting off any chance for real recovery. The A.A./N.A.-
based approach far outweighs any other, for it goes to the
deepest roots of the spiritual sickness of addiction, to
change the whole person in a fundamental and lasting
way.

I also believe that inpatient treatment has the best
chance for lasting success with most adolescents,
although innovative outpatient programs are springing
up here and there across the country and accumulating
some success. If I were looking at treatment for my
adolescent child, however, I would insist upon a proven
inpatient program, if at all possible, even if I had to travel
some distance.

If you are considering placing your youngster in a
specific treatment program, ask for names of people who
have been through the program and are willing to talk
about it. Don't be afraid to request verifiable information
about the facility's long-term success rate. As the
consumer, you have every right to know what you are
buying, in terms of your youngster's health.

9. Humbly and honestly, engage the help of whatever
   Higher Power you can claim. It may be God, Christ,
   Allah, the Great Spirit, or the Tao. It could be your

support group, this book, or even a slogan such as "Easy does it."

When you accept your powerlessness over the person and the problem and become willing to rely on something greater than yourself, new energy becomes available to you. What a relief it was when I could finally say, "I don't need to do it all! It's not all up to me! I can trust my situation to a greater source of strength."

Pray if you are able, honestly and simply, "I'm letting go; I'm willing to be led." Twenty minutes of quiet and inner stillness each day will put you back in touch with your own serenity. As you call on your Higher Power, you may not get the specific answer you hope for, but you *will* find strength—often in surprising places. A particular passage in your reading may touch you deeply. Another person may hold out a hand in loving concern, offer a hug, or say a word that lifts your spirit. *When we are fully surrendered, the creative energy of the universe becomes available to us.*

10. Begin to prepare your crisis plan for intervention. If you are dealing with true chemical dependency, the disease *will* progress, and there will be another crisis, and another, and another. Instead of dreading those crises, welcome them! Each one is an opportunity for transformation. You can use the next crisis to start turning things around!

How does one go about making a crisis plan?

—Gather as much information as possible about treatment centers and decide which is best for your family.
—Visit that center and enlist the help of its staff in your planning.

—Sit down with all members of your family (except the problem person) and decide on your bottom line. How far are you willing to go with this person and his or her illness before you can say "No farther," and mean it?

—Talk with school authorities, the person's employer, or both, if appropriate, and enlist their help. Emphasize that your family member may be suffering from a treatable disease, rather than a character defect, and you want to help rather than punish.

—Plan your proposed intervention in detail, if possible enlisting the help of a trained intervention specialist. Vernon Johnson's *Intervention: How to Help Someone Who Doesn't Want Help,* or his intervention chapter in *I'll Quit Tomorrow* can be a useful guide.

—Have an actual rehearsal of the intervention. Make sure everyone is in agreement with the plan before you take definitive action. Use the element of surprise to your advantage. Do *not* confront your problem person or let him or her know what's afoot until all elements of the plan are in place. Then you can present the person with positive options, such as going to treatment, or faithful attendance at A.A. or N.A. for a certain length of time (90 meetings in 90 days). Like Harlan's parents, you can even have the airline ticket in hand and the suitcase packed.

—In setting up your plan, be clear about the choices you can live with. What if the person refuses treatment? You must know what your next step will be. In our case, we would have told John he was on his own, for he was of age, had two years of college under his belt, and was able-bodied enough to work. We were no longer willing to support or live with someone who intended to remain sick, though we would continue to feel anxiety for him.

11. Watch for the next crisis, give thanks for it when it comes, then move ahead with your agreed-upon plan. Do not be swayed by promises your problem person may make at this point. You have already relied on far too many promises. It's time for deeds!

I offer some cautions here. About this time, you may begin to doubt the wisdom of your chosen plan of action; you may also feel a bit depressed, once the plan is set in motion. This is counterproductive thinking, which must be discounted. The offering of a chance for real, specific help is the most loving thing you can do for your problem person. Stick with the plan, based on your own best thinking and the advice of knowledgeable others, and move ahead confidently.

Your problem person may react to your decision in an angry, resentful manner. That's not important. This is not a parent-popularity contest, but a matter of life and death. *Chemical dependency is fatal if not treated.*

12. Finally, prepare for a new way of living as a family. Once the process of change is under way, everyone in the family will be called upon to adapt to the new situation. It won't be easy to give up old habits, even miserable ones, or to set aside old defenses, but the only way to become truly healthy is to relinquish everything sick.

The dominating mother who has tried to control the emotional life of the household will let go. The rebellious son who has been the focus of the family's anxiety will no longer keep everyone tied in knots. The preoccupied father who left discipline up to the mother will become a stronger parent. The lonely brother who covered up for his addicted sibling will chose honesty over misguided loyalty. The conscientious sister who wept for her family will dry her tears and find delight in her own individuality. The recovering addict will exercise self-discipline and live with occasional pain as he moves into the joys of recovery. All family members will share feelings and let others know what they need, still fully aware that the response is up to each individual and cannot be imposed by others.

For years, and even generations, we dysfunctional families have told ourselves that it is better to settle for the evil we know than to gamble on the evil we don't know. The smoke screen of chemical dependency dictates that attitude, but it is a defensive and fearful way to live, and it never leads to freedom.

In *Will and Spirit,* Gerald May describes addiction as "the sacred disease of the modern world." He explains:

> Addictions can be tragedies, but on occasion they can be gifts as well. Sooner or later in the terrible course of addiction one comes to what is called rock bottom. At this point one is forced either to reach out toward the wonderful mystery of life or to continue with a willfulness that will obviously end in death . . . [and] *we are all addicts* [emphasis added].

If you are not addicted to alcohol or other drugs, aren't you at least addicted to someone who is?

Each of us enters upon the way to wholeness only when we have become so utterly wretched that we are willing to risk a leap for life into the great unknown. In recovery, undreamed-of blessings await us. Weak and ineffectual though we may feel, we already have been given profound inner strengths and powerful potentials.

We *can* deal with life's challenges. We *can* claim our fulfillment and joy. *Today* is the day to begin!

# Support Groups and Resources

Alcoholics Anonymous
  General Service Office
468-470 Park Avenue South     *or:*   P.O. Box 459
New York, NY 10016                    New York, NY 10163
(212)686-1100

Al-Anon Family Groups
1372 Broadway
P.O. Box 862
Midtown Station
New York, NY 10118-0862
(212)302-7240

Cocaine Hotline
1-800-COCAINE

Families Anonymous
  World Service Office          *or:*   P.O. Box 528
14553 Delano Street, Suite 316        Van Nuys, CA 91408
Van Nuys, CA 91411
(818)989-7985

Narcotics Anonymous
  World Service Office
16155 Wyandotte St.
P.O. Box 9999
Van Nuys, CA 91409
(818)780-3951

Nar-Anon Family Groups
P.O. Box 2562
Palos Verdes, CA 90274
(213)547-5800

National Clearinghouse for
   Alcohol and Drug Information
Box 2345
Rockville, MD 20852
(301)468-2600

National Council on Alcoholism
12 West 12st St., 7th Flr.
New York, NY 10010
(212)206-6770

National Institute on
   Drug Abuse
5600 Fishers Lane
Rockville, MD 20857
(301)443-6480

# Reading List

*Alcoholics Anonymous*. 3rd rev. ed. New York: Alcoholics Anonymous World Services, 1976. The famous Big Book of A.A., a compendium of the Alcoholics Anonymous philosophy, with many inspiring stories by recovering alcoholics.

Stephen Apthorp. *Alcohol and Substance Abuse: A Clergy Handbook*. Wilton, Conn.: Morehouse-Barlow, 1986. A must for the bookshelf of clergy, in particular, and any helping professionals who deal with troubled families, by an author who thoroughly understands addiction and its effects on family and community.

Tilden Edwards. *Spiritual Friend*. New York: Paulist Press, 1980. An introduction to spiritual direction.

Gary G. Forrest. *How to Cope with a Teenage Drinker: New Alternatives and Hope for Parents and Families*. New York: Atheneum Publishers, 1983. A common-sense approach by an experienced counselor.

William Glasser. *Reality Therapy: A New Approach to Psychiatry*. New York: Harper & Row, 1984. A physician tells how to change sick attitudes through rewards for responsible behavior.

Michael Jackson and Bruce Jackson. *Doing Drugs*. New York: Saint Martin's/Marek, 1983. A graphic look at the realities of the adolescent drug culture.

Vernon E. Johnson. *I'll Quit Tomorrow*. rev. ed. New York: Harper & Row, 1980. The standard in chemical dependency. A ground-breaking examination of the disease, with specifics on a productive approach to recovery.

Vernon E. Johnson. *Intervention: How to Help Someone Who Doesn't Want Help*. New York: Harper & Row, 1987. A minister tells how intervention works, how to prepare for it, initiate it, and see it through.

Joseph L. Kellermann. Father Kellermann's many helpful publications for families of chemically dependent people include a series of inexpensive pamphlets published by Hazelden Educational Materials, Box 176, Pleasant Valley Rd., Center City, MN 55012. Some also are available in foreign-language editions:

*A.A.—A Family Affair*
*A Guide for the Family of the Alcoholic*
*Al-Anon: A Message of Hope*
*Alcoholism: A Merry-Go-Round Named Denial*
*The Family and Alcoholism:*
  *A Move from Pathology to Process*
*Grief: A Basic Reaction to Alcoholism*
*Reconciliation with God and Family*

Jean Kinney and Gwen Leaton. *Loosening the Grip: A Handbook of Alcohol Information*. St. Louis, Mo.: C. V. Mosby Co., 1983. Solid information by professionals, in an easy-to-read format.

George Mann. *Recovery of Reality: Overcoming Chemical Dependency*. New York: Harper & Row, 1979. The medical director of St. Mary's Rehabilitation Center in Minneapolis discusses the disease and its treatment.

Gerald May. *Addiction and Grace*. New York: Harper & Row, 1988. The best book available on the spiritual dimension of addiction and recovery, by a board-certified psychiatrist, the director for spiritual guidance at the Shalem Institute for Spiritual Formation, Washington, D.C.

Jack Mumey. *Sitting in the Bay Window: A Book for Parents of Young Alcoholics*. Chicago: Contemporary Books, 1984. Later edition retitled *Young Alcoholics: A Book for Parents*. 1986. Hard issues made easier by the author's compassion and lively sense of humor.

*Narcotics Anonymous*. 3rd ed. Van Nuys, Calif.: World Service Office, 1982. The basic text of Narcotics Anonymous, including many encouraging stories told by recovering addicts.

*One Day at a Time in Al-Anon*. New York: Al-Anon Family Group Headquarters, 1986. An excellent book of meditations for daily use by anyone concerned about another's use of alcohol or other drugs.

Philip Parham. *Letting God: Christian Meditations for Recovering Persons*. New York: Harper & Row, 1988. Fine daily readings for any Christian struggling with active addiction or its aftermath.

Beth Polson with Miller Newton. *Not My Kid: A Family's Guide to Kids and Drugs*. New York: Arbor House Publishing Co., 1984. Good descriptions of mood-altering chemicals and their effects. Useful vocabulary information.

John A. Sanford. *Dreams and Healing*. New York: Paulist Press, 1978.

William Steig. *Sylvester and the Magic Pebble*. New York: Windmill Books, 1969. A fable to remind us of the power of love.

David Toma with Irving N. Levey. *Toma Tells It Straight— With Love*. New York: Books in Focus, 1981. A former undercover cop gets down to basics about what drugs can do to young lives.

Sharon Wegscheider. *Another Chance: Hope and Health for Alcoholic Families*. Palo Alto, Calif.: Science and Behavior, 1980. The best book I know for families in recovery. Excellent chapter on intervention.

Sharon Wegscheider-Cruse. *Choice-Making*. Pompano Beach, Fla.: Health Communications, 1985. More recovery for families, especially adult children of alcoholics.

Phyllis York and David York, with Ted Wachtel. *Toughlove*. New York: Doubleday & Co., 1982. A parent's survival kit. Good, if you keep in mind that alcoholism/addiction are fatal diseases and diseases need appropriate treatment.

Many other excellent publications are available from Hazelden Educational Materials, Box 176, Pleasant Valley Rd., Center City, MN 55012.